THE ULTIMATE BOOK OF THE
HUMAN BODY

Claudia Martin

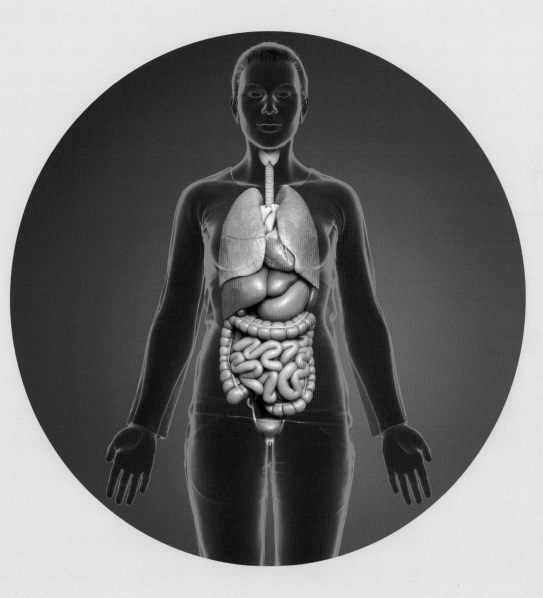

Consultant: Dr. Kristina Routh

ARCTURUS

Picture Credits:
Every attempt has been made to clear copyright. Should there be any inadvertent omission, please apply to the publisher for rectification.
Key: b–bottom, t–top, c–center, l–left, r–right

Alamy: 4b (Leonello Calvetti), 5 (Reuters), 25b (Folio Images), 36–37 (PCN Black), 41 (Westend61 GmbH), 42 (EyeEm), 49br (GL Archive), 56, 63 (Science Photo Library), 112 (Greatstock); **Andreas Vesalius:** 35br; **Bridgeman Images:** 12bl (Luisa Ricciarini), 13tr (Science and Society Picture Library), 13br, 79tr (Archives Charmet), 84c (NPL/DeA Picture Library); **Getty Images:** 12–13 (Jose Luis Pelaez Inc), 18 (Taiyou Nomachi), 22br (Ruslan Dashinsky), 29br (Gerasimov174), 51br (Mondadori Portfolio), 68br (Hinterhaus Productions), 101r (fstop123); **National Library of Medicine:** 82br; **Science Photo Library:** front cover (Roger Harris), 7, 27, 47, 67, 87, 107 (Pixologicstudio), 9br, 11tr, 39tr, 72, 113br (Steve GSchmeissner), 14, 79br, 110c (Mikkel Juul Jenson), 15br (A. Barrington Brown/Gonville & Caius College), 21 (Eye of Science), 26bl (Prof. P. Motta/A. Caggiati/University "La Sapienza", Rome), 34 (Dennis Kunkel Microscopy), 40br, 116cr (Science Photo), 48 (Alain Pol, ISM), 75br (M. I. Walker/Science Source), 80 (KH Fung), 81br (Microscape), 89t (James King-Holmes/Henry Luckhoo), 91c, 92–93c (Kemoal/BSIP), 95br, 104c (Fernando da Cunha), 118c (Jacopin); **Shutterstock:** 1 (SK Chavan), 6b, 20c, 29t (EreborMountain), 8, 75t (Tefi), 9tl, 9tr, 9cl, 9cr, 15cr, 17cr, 22cl, 60t, 61t, 62c, 73c, 75cl, 88, 109t (Designua), 9tc (Lopolo), 9tlb, 35c, 49c, 106cr (Aldona Griskeviciene), 9trb, 9cbr (Achiichiii), 9cbl (Art of Science), 10–11, 121c (Macrovector), 16c (kanyanat wongsa), 16bl (Anna Om), 17tr (Halfpoint), 17bl (Ysbrand Cosijn), 19tl (Aaron Amat), 19tr (Rido), 19cl (manams), 19clc (Ros Fraser), 19crc (LiuSol), 19cr (ChaosMaker), 20br, 30–31b (Monkey Business Images), 23t, 100bc (Shanvood), 23c (316pixel), 23br (Image Point Fr), 24tl (Flashon Studio), 24cl (Eric Eric), 24bc (pixelstock), 25tr (naluwan), 26c, 73br (SciePro), 28, 32, 37c, 50cr, 54t, 59l, 83t, 86 (VectorMine), 29c, 36cl (stihii), 30c (Wipark Kulniradorn), 30bl (Triff), 31tr (Radiological imaging), 31c (GagliardiPhotography), 33tr (Bizroug), 33cl (sciencepics), 33cr (ilusmedical), 33bl (OSTILL is Franck Camhi), 33br, 82c (La Gorda), 38c (Alexander_P), 38b (Marochkina Anastasiia), 38–39b (Subbotina Anna), 39cl Carlos E. Santa Maria), 39c (Syda Productions), 39br (T-Design), 40c (zuper_electracat), 43c (solar22), 43br (Fabio Principe), 44b (Belish), 45cl (alphabe), 45br (Kvitka Fabian), 46br, 54, 74 (Olga Bolbot), 50cl, 51t (GraphicsRF), 52–53 (Izf), 52cl (Drp8), 53c (Amadeu Blasco), 55br (Cat Simpson), 57c, 114cr (Sakurra), 57br (ChaNaWiT), 58cr (Vector-3D), 58bl (Jezper), 58br (Sungthong), 59br (Tacio Philip Sansonovski), 60c (Djordje Raca), 60bl (Samo Trebizan), 60br, 89c (LDarin), 61cl (extender_01), 61br (Alpha Tauri 3D Graphics), 62br (Doidam 10), 64cr (Hong Vo), 64cl (PRILL), 64–65b (5 second Studio), 65tr Juergen Faelchle), 65c (Danut Vieru), 65br (Rob Byron), 66br (Olena758), 68c, 69t (stockshoppe), 69c (medicalstocks), 69br (Microgen), 70 (oNabby), 71 (elenabsl), 75cr (keerati), 76c, 113c (Pikovit), 76br (Monet_3K), 77 (Graphic Photo Art-MomPhoto), 78–79 (UfaBizPhoto), 81c (Andrea Danti), 83b, 102br (Antonio Guillem), 84–85 (narikan), 85tr (Deborah Asamoah), 89br (Jose Luis Calvo), 90 (Air Images), 91br (SpeedKingz), 92cl (Jeka), 92br (Marlon Lopez MMG1 Design), 93tr, 95tl (Ermolaev Alexander), 93cr (Samuel Borges Photography), 93br (Ollyy), 94 (Dragon Images), 96cr, 99c, 102c (decade 3D - anatomy online), 96br (buteo), 97 (rawpixel.com), 98 (zhukovvlad), 99br (cowardlion), 101tl (Shopping King Louie), 103, 105br, 124–125b (fizkes), 105tr (Ilike), 108cu (Anuwat Meereewee), 108br (Peter Hermes Furian), 109b (Anatoly Tiplyashin), 110–111 (KI Petro), 111t (Nitikran Photography), 111br (Vikafoto33), 114br (AS Foodstudio), 115 (Lapina), 116cl (Maxx-Studio), 116br (Andrey Popov), 117t (miha de), 117b (Celig), 118–119 (Impact Photography), 120 (DGL Images), 121br (vectorfusionart), 122c (Eduards Normaals), 122br (peakstock), 123bl (michaeljung), 123br (espies), 124c (Win Win Artlab), 125tl (Leremy). **Cover illustrations** all Shutterstock: front cover (martan) back cover centre (Luis Molinero), back cover left and right, front flap (Master1305), back flap (GraphicsRF.com).

ARCTURUS

ISBN: 978-1-3988-1536-0
CH007798US
Supplier 29, Date 0622, PI 00000668

Printed in China

Author: Claudia Martin
Designer: Lorraine Inglis
Consultant: Dr. Kristina Routh
Editor: Becca Clunes
Design manager: Jessica Holliland
Managing editor: Joe Harris

In this book, one billion means one thousand million (1,000,000,000) and one trillion means one million million (1,000,000,000,000).

THE ULTIMATE BOOK OF THE
HUMAN BODY

CONTENTS

THE HUMAN BODY

There are nearly 8 billion people on Earth, each with an extraordinary body, different from any other. Your body enables you to play games, paint pictures, sing songs, or hug the people you love. Although modern humans have lived on Earth for 350,000 years, we are still solving the mysteries of our wonderful bodies.

An anatomist is a scientist who studies the structure of the human body and all its parts. It is because of the careful, centuries-long work of anatomists that we understand the structure of the heart, its strong-muscled walls and sensitive nerves. Anatomists work with other scientists, called physiologists, who delve into how structures work. They make sense of how the heart's muscles tighten, pumping blood through tubes called blood vessels.

If someone's heart were struggling to pump blood to every toe and finger, they would seek the help of a doctor, also known as a physician. Doctors study anatomy and physiology, as well as diseases and their latest treatments. A doctor who specializes in treating the heart, called a cardiologist, might give their particular advice. A physiotherapist could join the team, suggesting exercises to strengthen the heart. A change in diet might be suggested by a nutritionist, who studies how the food we eat affects our health.

For centuries, people thought the heart was where thoughts and love were born. Today, we know that the brain is the home of ideas and emotions. We have come to this understanding through the work of scientists who study the structure and activity of the brain, known as neuroscientists. They watch electrical signals travel along tiny neurons, creating ideas and feelings from poetry to sums and worry to joy. However, it is yet another group of scientists, called psychologists, who try to understand what events and memories can trigger laughter or tears. Today, they can even tell you why the smell of chocolate cake reminds you of a friend or a forgotten place.

Discovering the human body's astounding parts and workings, its surprising skills and senses, helps you to understand and care for it—and to enjoy being the breathing, thinking, laughing you.

Every day, the average heart beats 100,000 times. Over your life, your heart will probably beat more than 2.5 billion times.

Wheelchair basketballers battle for the ball during a match between the United States and Germany.

Chapter 1

BUILDING BLOCKS FOR LIFE

Like the home you live in, your body is made of a series of building blocks. However, while your home might be made of clay, which forms bricks, which in turn build walls, your body is made of cells, which form tissues, which in turn build organs. All these building blocks come together to make the one and only you!

Like everything else on Earth, your body's tiniest building blocks are atoms. Your body contains something in the region of 3 octillion atoms (3 followed by 28 zeros). Scientists know of 118 different types of atoms, such as hydrogen and carbon. Around half of those types are found in your body. More than 65 percent of your body is oxygen atoms. Other atoms found in large quantities are carbon, hydrogen, and nitrogen, followed by much smaller quantities of atoms such as calcium and phosphorus.

Most atoms in your body are linked to other atoms to form groups of atoms called molecules. For example, most of the oxygen atoms in your body are linked to hydrogen atoms to form water molecules. Molecules group together to form larger building blocks, called cells. Your body contains around 30 trillion cells (3 followed by 13 zeros). Your cells are busy, working parts. They produce their own energy so they can carry out work such as making materials. There are more than 200 different types of cells, such as skin cells and bone cells, each with their own special job to do.

Similar cells group together to form materials called tissues, such as skin or bone. Different types of tissue are grouped together to form structures called organs, such as the brain or stomach. An organ is dedicated to carrying out a particular job or jobs. For example, the stomach's job is to mix and mush food. Organs work together or with other tissues to form organ systems. Along with organs such as the intestines and liver, the stomach is part of the digestive system, which breaks down food. Your organ systems work together to make a complete human being—you.

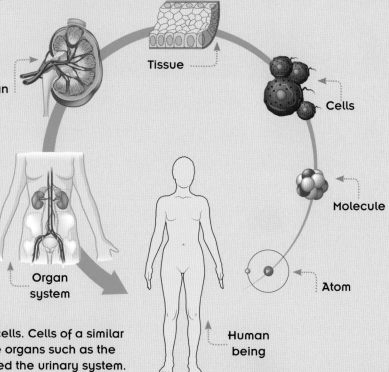

Atoms form molecules, which group together into cells. Cells of a similar type make tissues, which group together to make organs such as the kidney. The kidney is part of an organ system called the urinary system.

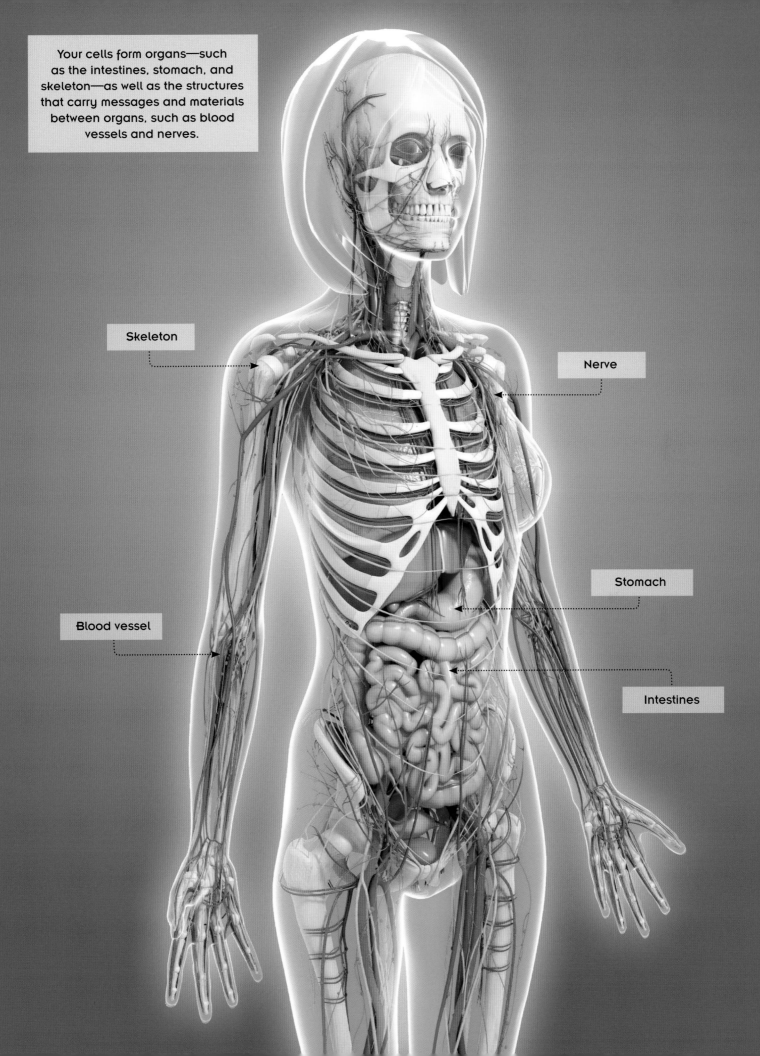

Your cells form organs—such as the intestines, stomach, and skeleton—as well as the structures that carry messages and materials between organs, such as blood vessels and nerves.

Skeleton

Nerve

Stomach

Blood vessel

Intestines

CELLS

Cells are your body's smallest working parts. The tiniest of them are just 0.0004 cm (0.00016 in) across. Your body contains around 220 different types of cells, with different shapes, different jobs, and the ability to make different materials. However, most cells contain the same structures, including a nucleus, which acts as the "brain" of the cell. Similar cells group together to form tissue.

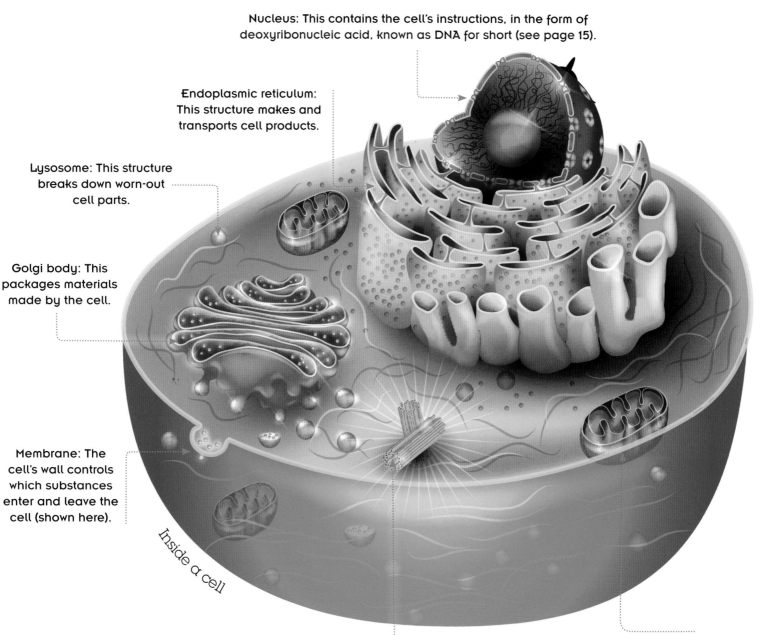

Nucleus: This contains the cell's instructions, in the form of deoxyribonucleic acid, known as DNA for short (see page 15).

Endoplasmic reticulum: This structure makes and transports cell products.

Lysosome: This structure breaks down worn-out cell parts.

Golgi body: This packages materials made by the cell.

Membrane: The cell's wall controls which substances enter and leave the cell (shown here).

Inside a cell

Centriole: When it is time to make a new cell, to replace old cells or to enable the body to grow, centrioles help the cell to divide into two or more new cells (see page 17).

Mitochondrion: This structure uses glucose sugar (from the food we eat) and oxygen (from the air we breathe) to make energy so the cell can carry out its work.

Connective tissue

Connective tissue is found between other tissues in the body. It includes bone, fat, and cartilage.

Bone cell

Fat cell

The body is made of four main types of tissue: connective, nervous, epithelial, and muscle.

Nervous tissue

Nervous tissue forms the brain and nerves. It is composed of different types of nerve cells, also called neurons, and glial cells.

Nerve cell

Glial cell

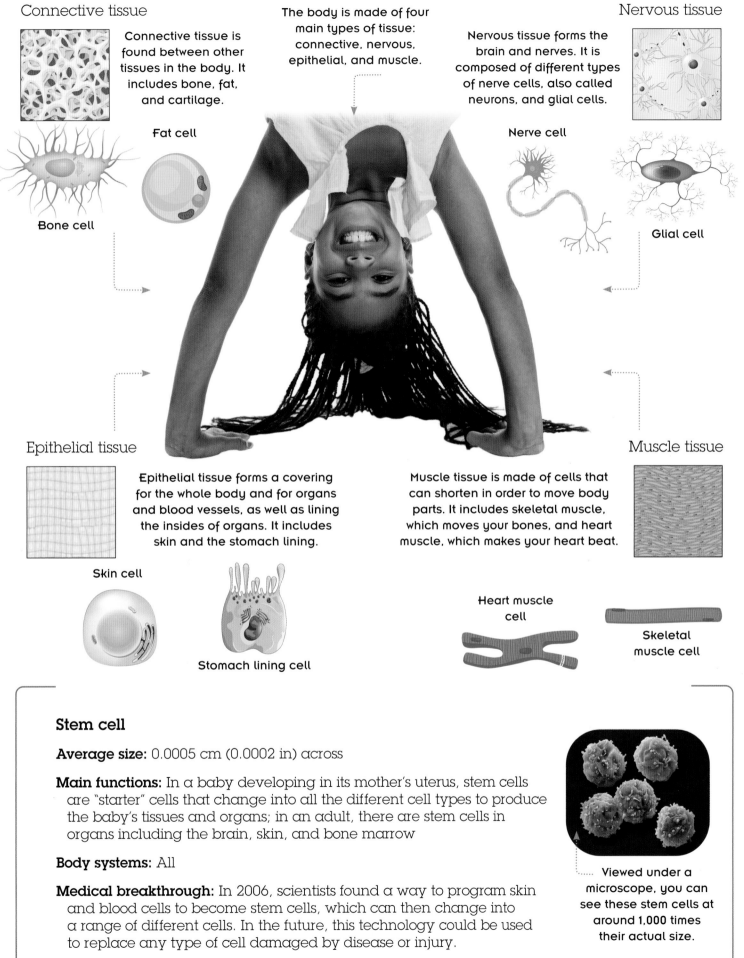

Epithelial tissue

Epithelial tissue forms a covering for the whole body and for organs and blood vessels, as well as lining the insides of organs. It includes skin and the stomach lining.

Skin cell

Stomach lining cell

Muscle tissue

Muscle tissue is made of cells that can shorten in order to move body parts. It includes skeletal muscle, which moves your bones, and heart muscle, which makes your heart beat.

Heart muscle cell

Skeletal muscle cell

Stem cell

Average size: 0.0005 cm (0.0002 in) across

Main functions: In a baby developing in its mother's uterus, stem cells are "starter" cells that change into all the different cell types to produce the baby's tissues and organs; in an adult, there are stem cells in organs including the brain, skin, and bone marrow

Body systems: All

Medical breakthrough: In 2006, scientists found a way to program skin and blood cells to become stem cells, which can then change into a range of different cells. In the future, this technology could be used to replace any type of cell damaged by disease or injury.

Viewed under a microscope, you can see these stem cells at around 1,000 times their actual size.

ORGAN SYSTEMS

An organ is a body structure with vital work to carry out. Most doctors agree you have around 78 organs, ranging from the smallest—the pineal gland in your brain, just 7 mm (0.3 in) across—to the largest, your skin. Organs work together with other organs and tissues to form organ systems. The organs are usually grouped into 11 organ systems.

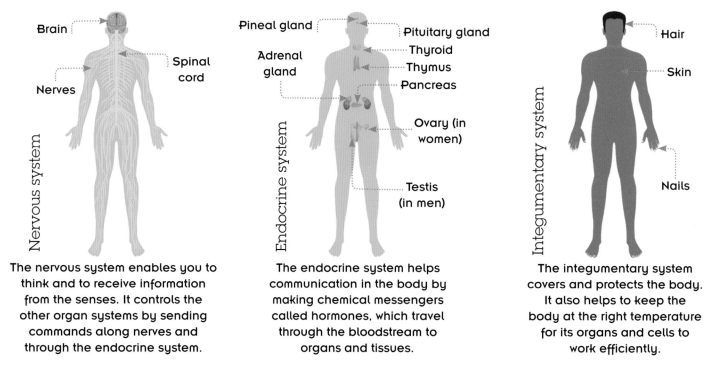

Nervous system

Brain
Spinal cord
Nerves

The nervous system enables you to think and to receive information from the senses. It controls the other organ systems by sending commands along nerves and through the endocrine system.

Endocrine system

Pineal gland
Adrenal gland
Pituitary gland
Thyroid
Thymus
Pancreas
Ovary (in women)
Testis (in men)

The endocrine system helps communication in the body by making chemical messengers called hormones, which travel through the bloodstream to organs and tissues.

Integumentary system

Hair
Skin
Nails

The integumentary system covers and protects the body. It also helps to keep the body at the right temperature for its organs and cells to work efficiently.

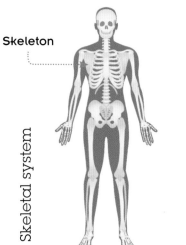

Skeletal system

Skeleton

The skeletal system provides your body with support, helps you move, and protects your most vital organs. Bones also make blood cells and store useful materials.

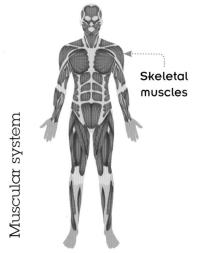

Muscular system

Skeletal muscles

The muscular system works with the skeletal system so you can move. Different types of muscle also make the heart beat and make organs such as the stomach squeeze and relax.

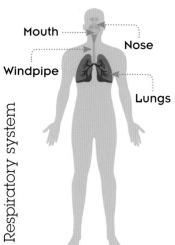

Respiratory system

Mouth
Nose
Windpipe
Lungs

The respiratory system draws air into the lungs to supply your cells with oxygen, which they use to produce energy. The system also expels a waste product of making energy: carbon dioxide.

II

Pancreas

Average adult weight: 90 g (3 oz)

Main functions: Making chemicals, called enzymes, that break down food and releasing them into the intestines, and making hormones and releasing them into the blood

Body systems: Digestive and endocrine

Medical breakthrough: The pancreas was first identified by the ancient Greek surgeon Herophilos (335–280 BCE).

Magnified around 1,500 times and tinted to make it clearer, a cell in the pancreas is at work. Its golgi apparatus (yellow strands) is packaging enzymes in round parcels called vesicles (red balls) before they are exported from the cell.

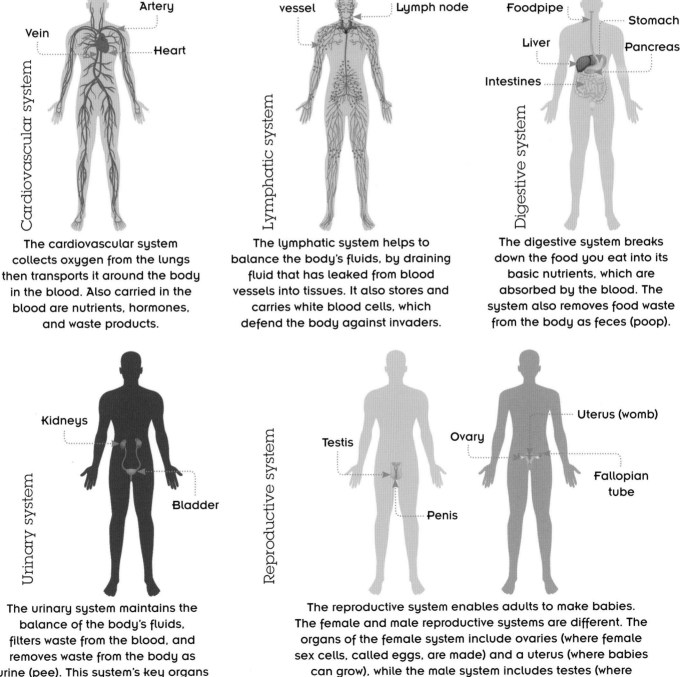

Cardiovascular system

Vein · Artery · Heart

The cardiovascular system collects oxygen from the lungs then transports it around the body in the blood. Also carried in the blood are nutrients, hormones, and waste products.

Lymphatic system

Lymph vessel · Lymph node

The lymphatic system helps to balance the body's fluids, by draining fluid that has leaked from blood vessels into tissues. It also stores and carries white blood cells, which defend the body against invaders.

Digestive system

Foodpipe · Stomach · Liver · Pancreas · Intestines

The digestive system breaks down the food you eat into its basic nutrients, which are absorbed by the blood. The system also removes food waste from the body as feces (poop).

Urinary system

Kidneys · Bladder

The urinary system maintains the balance of the body's fluids, filters waste from the blood, and removes waste from the body as urine (pee). This system's key organs are the kidneys and bladder.

Reproductive system

Testis · Penis · Ovary · Uterus (womb) · Fallopian tube

The reproductive system enables adults to make babies. The female and male reproductive systems are different. The organs of the female system include ovaries (where female sex cells, called eggs, are made) and a uterus (where babies can grow), while the male system includes testes (where male sex cells, called sperm, are made) and a penis.

MAGIC TO MEDICINE

Medicine is the science of keeping people healthy and helping the sick. Today, medicine is carried out by highly trained doctors, nurses, and other professionals. In the past, people turned to herbal healers, magicians, and even cheats and tricksters.

Today, medicine is a science, based on study, experiment, and fact. In ancient times, healing was not usually treated as a science. Many people believed that disease was brought by the gods, evil spirits, or bad air. In ancient civilizations such as Babylon and Egypt, healers often recited magic spells or prayed to the gods. However, many early healers also knew how to deliver babies, set broken bones, and choose herbs to make effective medicines. A large number of modern medicines are still made with chemicals that come from plants, including the Madagascar periwinkle, which helps treat cancer, and the opium poppy, which can ease pain.

Herbal medicine

A 13th-century Italian illustration shows how to make a herbal medicine.

The ancient Greek doctor Hippocrates (c.460–370 BCE) believed that illness had a physical cause. He was a great influence on later doctors. Like today's doctors, he diagnosed (identified the nature of) an illness after carefully observing his patients and taking note of their symptoms (evidence of disease, such as fever or swelling). The next centuries saw the founding of many medical schools and close study of the human body, but medicine remained hit-and-miss for hundreds of years. Even in the early 20th century, sick people might turn to someone who sold "medicine" that promised much but did more harm than good.

This cartoon from 1830 makes fun of a wandering medicine seller, who went house to house selling pills and potions he made himself.

Medicine seller

Today, a doctor may use a stethoscope to amplify (make louder) sounds inside the body, made by the heart, lungs, and intestines.

During the 19th century, doctors started to use microscopes to study microorganisms such as bacteria. They began to understand that some illnesses—from food poisoning to malaria and cholera—are caused by microorganisms. As a result, many governments focused on providing sewers and clean running water, which are essential to prevent the spread of some diseases. Study of atoms, molecules, and cells led to the development of new medicines. Today, medicines can: destroy microorganisms, such as antibiotics that kill bacteria; replace missing substances in the body, such as vitamins or hormones; treat cancer by stopping cancerous cells from dividing; or target the brain, which doctors now know controls the body systems.

In the 19th century, popular medicines might contain poisons such as arsenic, lead, and mercury.

Potions and pills

A strand of DNA unzips in a cell's nucleus
(turquoise sphere) and is copied by a strand
of RNA, which leaves the nucleus and gives
the instruction to make new materials.

DNA

Your cells know what to do because of instructions contained in DNA, which is short for deoxyribonucleic acid. We often call these instructions genes. Your genes give instructions for what materials your cells make, how your organs work, and how you look.

DNA is found inside the nucleus of nearly every cell in your body. The DNA in each cell is nearly identical to the DNA in every other cell. DNA is a very complex molecule made of two strands that wrap around each other to form a twisting ladder shape. The rungs of the ladder are made of four chemicals called bases. These are adenine, thymine, cytosine, and guanine. Your DNA contains around 3 billion of these four bases.

If you view DNA as a language, the four bases are its letters. A combination of "letters" spells out a "word," which is an individual gene. A gene usually gives instructions for making a particular material the body needs. Your DNA contains 20,000 to 25,000 genes, some of them containing a few hundred bases and some up to 2 million bases.

DNA cannot leave the cell nucleus, which is where this all-important molecule is safest. When an instruction to make a protein needs to be taken to a structure in the rest of the cell, a molecule called RNA (short for ribonucleic acid) steps in. The portion of DNA containing that particular gene unzips itself from the other half of the ladder. The RNA copies the DNA's bases and leaves the nucleus through a tiny hole called a pore.

The base thymine always pairs with adenine, while guanine always pairs with cytosine.

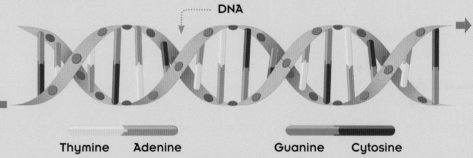

DNA

| Thymine | Adenine | | Guanine | Cytosine |

DNA

Length of DNA in each cell: 2 m (6.6 ft)

Main functions: Carrying instructions for development, growth, functioning, and reproduction

Body systems: All

Medical breakthrough: The twisting-ladder shape of DNA, also called a double helix, was discovered in 1953 by scientists James Watson and Francis Crick, drawing on earlier work by Rosalind Franklin and others.

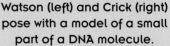

Watson (left) and Crick (right) pose with a model of a small part of a DNA molecule.

CHROMOSOMES

If DNA floated freely in the cell nucleus, it would get tangled! Instead, each molecule of DNA is coiled into a structure called a chromosome. You have 23 pairs of chromosomes in most of your cells, one half of each pair inherited from your mother and the other half from your father.

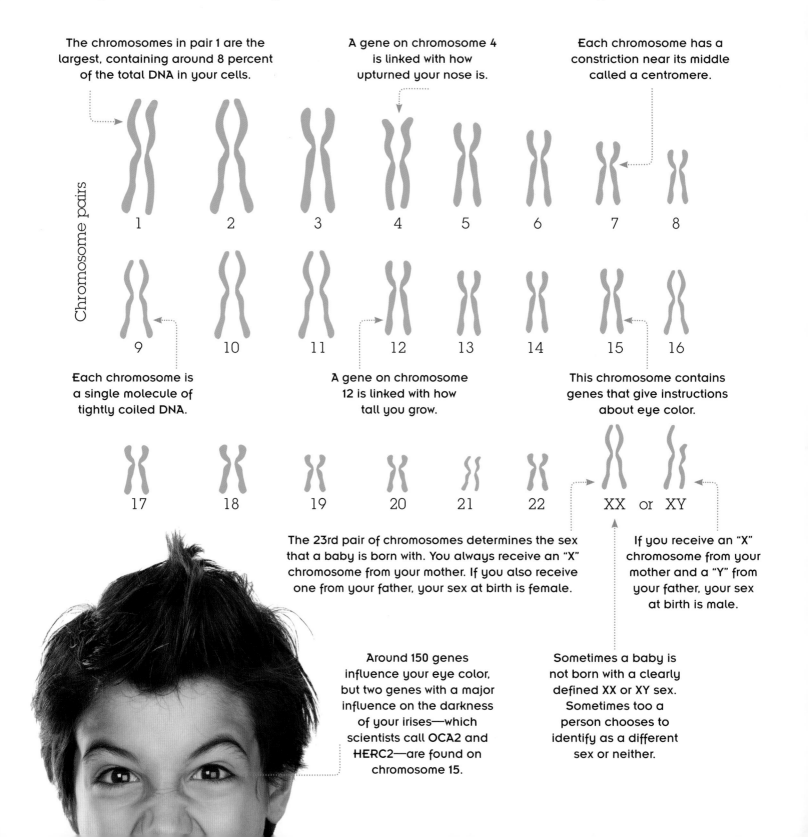

The chromosomes in pair 1 are the largest, containing around 8 percent of the total DNA in your cells.

A gene on chromosome 4 is linked with how upturned your nose is.

Each chromosome has a constriction near its middle called a centromere.

Chromosome pairs

1 2 3 4 5 6 7 8

9 10 11 12 13 14 15 16

Each chromosome is a single molecule of tightly coiled DNA.

A gene on chromosome 12 is linked with how tall you grow.

This chromosome contains genes that give instructions about eye color.

17 18 19 20 21 22 XX or XY

The 23rd pair of chromosomes determines the sex that a baby is born with. You always receive an "X" chromosome from your mother. If you also receive one from your father, your sex at birth is female.

If you receive an "X" chromosome from your mother and a "Y" from your father, your sex at birth is male.

Around 150 genes influence your eye color, but two genes with a major influence on the darkness of your irises—which scientists call OCA2 and HERC2—are found on chromosome 15.

Sometimes a baby is not born with a clearly defined XX or XY sex. Sometimes too a person chooses to identify as a different sex or neither.

Y chromosome

Average size when tightly coiled: 0.00005 cm (0.00002 in) long

Main functions: Determining whether a person is born with male or female reproductive organs

Body system: Reproductive

Medical breakthrough: In 2013, researchers discovered—through studying people's genes and the differences between them—that everyone with a Y chromosome is descended from one man who lived around 340,000 years ago.

Y chromosomes are passed only from father to son.

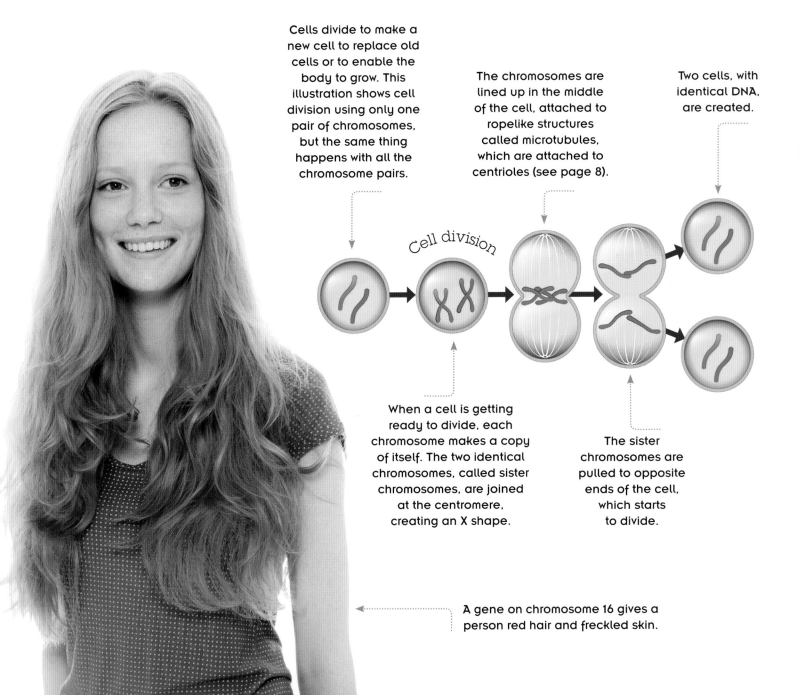

Cells divide to make a new cell to replace old cells or to enable the body to grow. This illustration shows cell division using only one pair of chromosomes, but the same thing happens with all the chromosome pairs.

The chromosomes are lined up in the middle of the cell, attached to ropelike structures called microtubules, which are attached to centrioles (see page 8).

Two cells, with identical DNA, are created.

Cell division

When a cell is getting ready to divide, each chromosome makes a copy of itself. The two identical chromosomes, called sister chromosomes, are joined at the centromere, creating an X shape.

The sister chromosomes are pulled to opposite ends of the cell, which starts to divide.

A gene on chromosome 16 gives a person red hair and freckled skin.

INHERITANCE

Inheritance is the process through which genes are passed from parents to their children. Inheritance is the reason why a person looks quite like their birth parents. Yet it also explains why you are not an identical copy of your mother, father, or siblings!

More than 99 percent of your genes are the same as every other human's, which is why humans have a great deal in common. It is the remaining less than 1 percent that makes you different: You may have blue eyes, straight red hair, and short legs while your friend has brown eyes, curly brown hair, and long legs. You share more DNA with your relatives than with other people, which is why you probably look quite like your birth family.

Half of your chromosomes came from your mother, in the egg that grew into you; while the other half came from your father, in the sperm that met that egg. Unlike all the other cells in the human body, egg and sperm cells have only one copy of each chromosome, not two copies. That single set of chromosomes is a random mix of the two copies of each chromosome that a mother or father received from their own parents. This mixing up, called recombination, explains why children of the same parents do not look identical to each other.

Identical twins develop from the same sperm and egg, so they share nearly all their DNA, making them the same sex and almost identical in appearance. In contrast, fraternal twins develop from different eggs and sperm, so they may be different sexes and look as different as any other siblings.

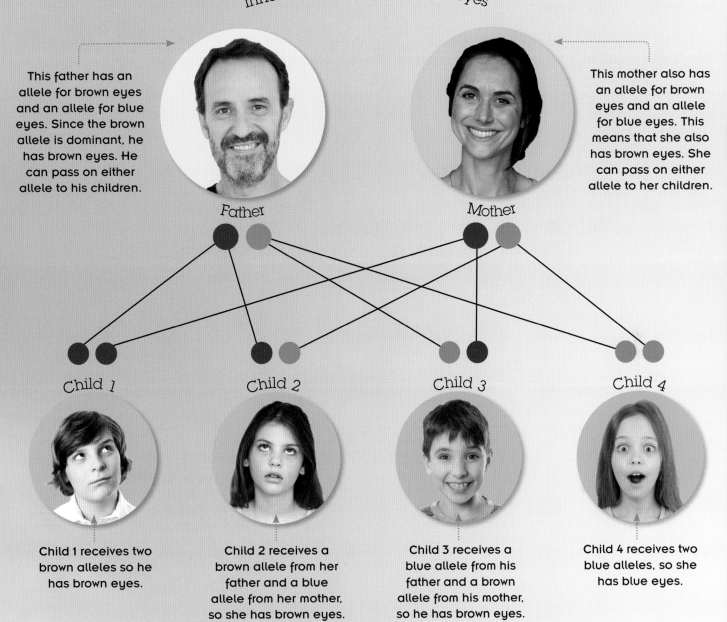

Inheritance of brown or blue eyes

This father has an allele for brown eyes and an allele for blue eyes. Since the brown allele is dominant, he has brown eyes. He can pass on either allele to his children.

This mother also has an allele for brown eyes and an allele for blue eyes. This means that she also has brown eyes. She can pass on either allele to her children.

Father

Mother

Child 1

Child 2

Child 3

Child 4

Child 1 receives two brown alleles so he has brown eyes.

Child 2 receives a brown allele from her father and a blue allele from her mother, so she has brown eyes.

Child 3 receives a blue allele from his father and a brown allele from his mother, so he has brown eyes.

Child 4 receives two blue alleles, so she has blue eyes.

When the egg and sperm have met, the new baby's cells have 23 pairs of chromosomes. Each chromosome in a pair contains the same set of genes, but the chromosome from the mother may have different versions, or alleles, of each gene from the versions in the father's chromosome. For example, the mother's genes for eye color may instruct for blue eyes, but the father's may instruct for brown eyes. In this case, it is the father's allele that will "win" because the allele for brown eyes is dominant, which means it is stronger and needs only one allele for it to show its effect. In contrast, the allele for blue eyes is recessive, which means there have to be two copies of the allele for it to be expressed. Skin shade is determined by several genes, but the genes that instruct for either dark or light skin cannot show dominance over each other. This is why children often—but not always—have a skin shade somewhere between those of their parents.

EGG

Every month, during a woman's reproductive years, she releases an egg. If the egg is fertilized by a sperm, it can develop into a baby. Eggs form in a woman's ovaries, while sperm are made in a man's testes.

A woman has two glands called ovaries, where eggs are stored until they mature. Once a month, women usually release a mature egg, which travels along one of the fallopian tubes toward the uterus, also called the womb. If the egg does not meet a sperm before it arrives in the uterus, the unfertilized egg is shed from the body along with the lining of the uterus. This monthly process of shedding the uterus lining is called menstruation, or "having a period."

The menstrual fluid is a mixture of blood and the uterus lining and might fill 6 to 8 teaspoons over around 5 days. Girls may start to menstruate between the ages of 9 and 16, but everyone's body is different. When a girl baby is born, her ovaries already house around a million immature eggs, but only 300 to 400 will be released over her life. Between the ages of around 45 and 55, a woman stops releasing eggs.

A man can release semen through their penis. Semen is a mixture of sperm and fluid. A sperm is around 0.005 cm (0.002 in) long. It has a tail, which makes a wavelike motion that enables it to swim through the uterus and up a fallopian tube. Boys may start to produce sperm between the ages of 9 and 15.

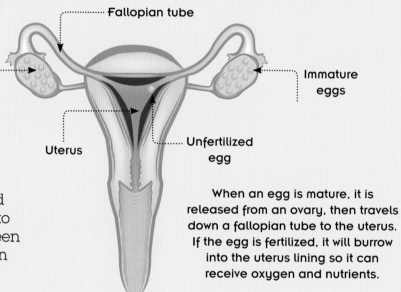

Fallopian tube

Ovary

Immature eggs

Uterus

Unfertilized egg

When an egg is mature, it is released from an ovary, then travels down a fallopian tube to the uterus. If the egg is fertilized, it will burrow into the uterus lining so it can receive oxygen and nutrients.

Egg

Average size: 0.01 cm (0.004 in) across

Main functions: Carrying the mother's chromosomes; and, if fertilized, providing food for the developing baby for the first few days

Body system: Reproductive

Medical breakthrough: In 1978, the world's first baby conceived by in vitro fertilization (IVF), named Louise Joy Brown, was born in England to parents Lesley and Peter Brown. In IVF, an egg is removed from the mother's ovaries and fertilized with sperm in a laboratory, then returned to the mother's uterus to grow.

IVF helps people with fertility problems to have a baby.

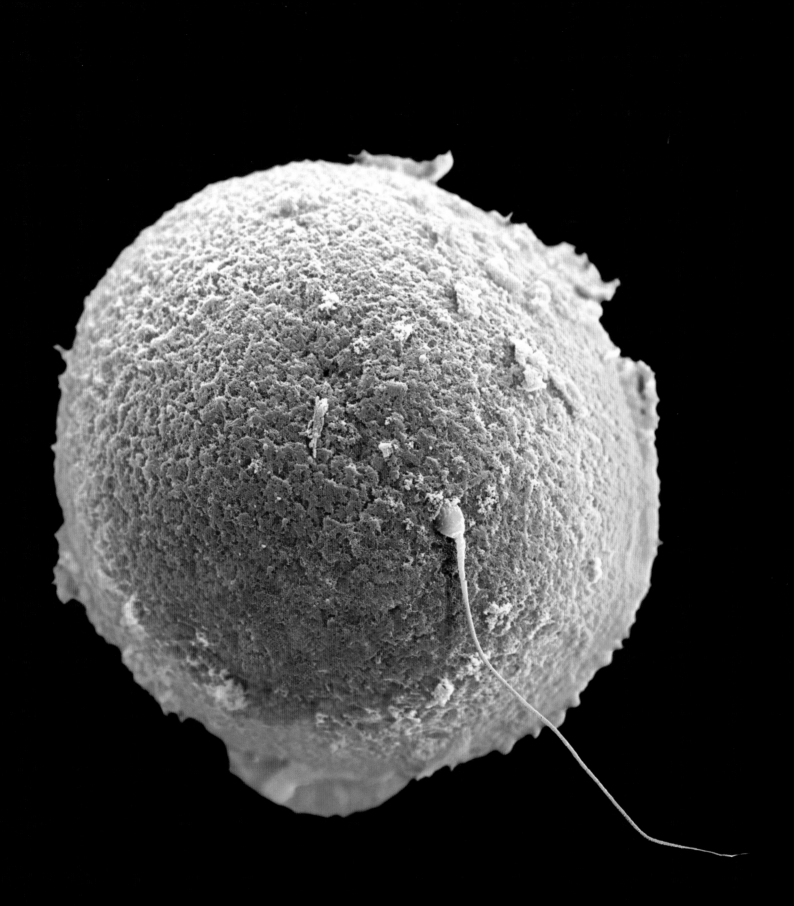

Many years after starting to produce eggs or sperm, an adult may feel ready to start a family. A powerful microscope has captured the moment when a sperm fertilizes an egg.

DEVELOPING BABY

A baby spends around nine months growing and developing inside its mother's uterus. Most babies are born around 40 weeks from the start of their mother's last menstruation, but many enter the world a little earlier or later.

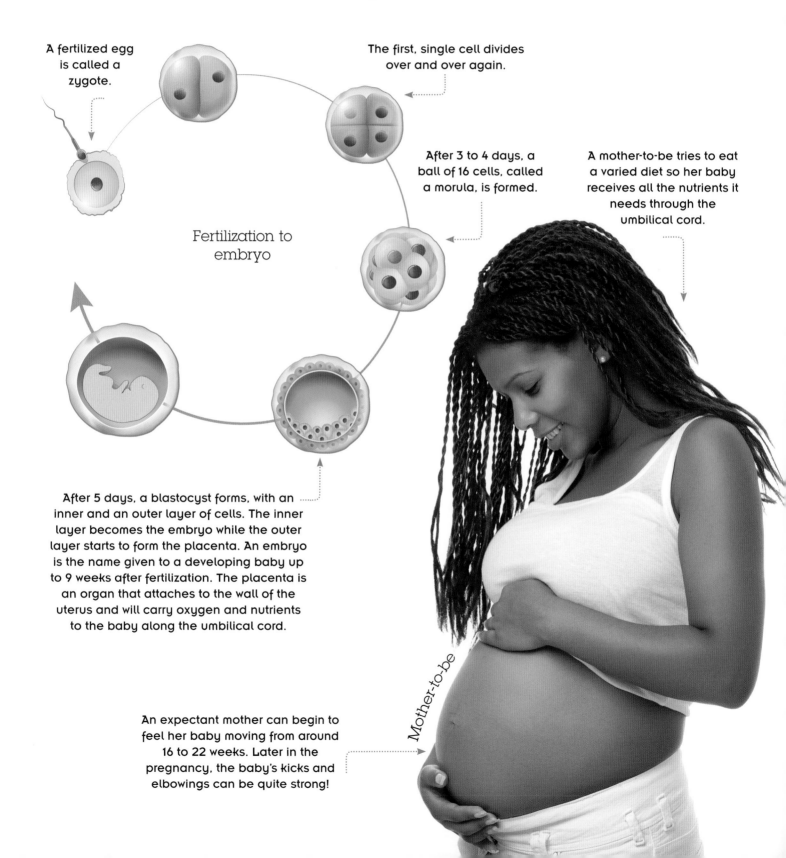

A fertilized egg is called a zygote.

The first, single cell divides over and over again.

After 3 to 4 days, a ball of 16 cells, called a morula, is formed.

A mother-to-be tries to eat a varied diet so her baby receives all the nutrients it needs through the umbilical cord.

Fertilization to embryo

After 5 days, a blastocyst forms, with an inner and an outer layer of cells. The inner layer becomes the embryo while the outer layer starts to form the placenta. An embryo is the name given to a developing baby up to 9 weeks after fertilization. The placenta is an organ that attaches to the wall of the uterus and will carry oxygen and nutrients to the baby along the umbilical cord.

Mother-to-be

An expectant mother can begin to feel her baby moving from around 16 to 22 weeks. Later in the pregnancy, the baby's kicks and elbowings can be quite strong!

Nine months of pregnancy

1 month: The embryo's heart is starting to form.

2 months: The umbilical cord is fully formed and the embryo is surrounded by a protective cushion of watery liquid called amniotic fluid.

3 months: The baby, now called a fetus, has all its organs as well as fingers and toes.

4 months: The fetus can pee, releasing its urine into the amniotic fluid.

5 months: Now the fetus can hear sounds outside the uterus and may "startle" at loud noises.

6 months: The fetus is covered with soft, fine hair called lanugo, which will be lost within a week or two of birth.

7 months: The fetus may suck its thumb as it gains fat and its lungs strengthen.

8 months: The fetus's eyes respond to light shining through the mother's skin and tissue.

9 months: Most babies, but not all, have turned head down ready for birth, as the round head will travel most smoothly through the mother's birth canal.

Newborn baby

A newborn can hear, smell, taste, and feel. Its eyes can only focus on objects up to 25 cm (10 in) away, which is the distance of its parents' faces when it is held.

Its main form of communication is crying, which it does to show it is hot, cold, tired, hungry for milk, or wants a cuddle.

Uterus (also called a womb)

Average size: 10 cm by 6 cm (4 in by 2.5 in) when not carrying a baby

Main functions: Nourishing and protecting a developing baby before birth, and contracting during birth to ease a baby into the world

Body system: Reproductive

Medical breakthrough: Between 16 and 36 weeks, the height of the uterus in centimeters is roughly equal to the fetus's age in weeks. This relationship was noted by doctor Ellice McDonald in 1906.

Medical professionals measure a mother-to-be's uterus to check on her baby's growth.

STAGES OF LIFE

Your body changes throughout life, during the fast-growing years of childhood and adolescence and into adulthood and old age. Your rate of learning is fastest in the first three years of life, but the process of gaining skills and knowledge continues through every year. Most elderly people say that age brings wisdom and strength of mind.

Human newborn babies are the most helpless of all baby animals, unable to hold up their head or co-ordinate their movements. By the age of two, the brain has tripled in weight since birth. Many children are able to use 300 words and understand hundreds more.

By the age of seven, the brain has reached 95 percent of its final weight. The early school years are a time of rapid learning, not just in reading, writing, mathematics, and sports, but also in building friendships and working together with others. Most children are now able to view the world from another's point of view.

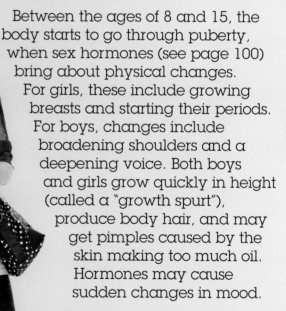

By the age of two, most children are able to walk and to throw a ball, but not yet catch it.

Many seven-year-olds have developed the co-ordination and balance needed to play ball sports or learn ballet.

Between the ages of 8 and 15, the body starts to go through puberty, when sex hormones (see page 100) bring about physical changes. For girls, these include growing breasts and starting their periods. For boys, changes include broadening shoulders and a deepening voice. Both boys and girls grow quickly in height (called a "growth spurt"), produce body hair, and may get pimples caused by the skin making too much oil. Hormones may cause sudden changes in mood.

As teenagers begin to search for independence, some may come into conflict with their parents.

By the age of 18, most people have grown to their full height. The brain has fully developed its ability to plan and to control emotions by around the age of 25. However, the ability to pay attention continues to improve until the age of 45. Adults may choose to form romantic relationships or to start a family. Adulthood brings greater freedoms as well as greater responsibilities, about work, money, and family.

Our cells can divide (see page 17) only 50 to 70 times. When there are not enough new cells to replace dead cells, tissues and organs begin to work less well. Cell division slows from the age of 30, but the effects are not usually felt for many more years. Elderly people may experience wrinkled skin, whitening hair, worsening hearing and sight, and more painful joints.

Until the age of around 50, your brain continues to improve its ability to use words and facts to back up arguments.

Taking regular exercise, eating a varied diet, and enjoying the company of family and friends can slow the aging process, helping us to feel healthier for longer.

Chapter 2

BODY STRUCTURE

Without your skeleton, you would be a sluglike blob. It is bones that give your body structure, while also protecting your organs. Working with your muscles, bones enable you to move. Wrapping the whole human-body package is the skin, which protects you, stops you from drying out, and helps you feel your surroundings.

Your bones make up your skeletal system. Most adults have 206 bones, but babies are born with over 300. Some of those bones—including many in the skull, arms, and legs—fuse together as you grow. The largest bone is the thigh bone, also called the femur. In an average adult man, it is 48 cm (19 in) long. The smallest bone is the stapes in the middle ear, just 0.25 cm (0.1 in) long.

Muscles form the muscular system. Since muscles and bones work together, their two body systems are often grouped together as the musculoskeletal system. The muscles that help to move bones are called skeletal muscles. There are more than 650 skeletal muscles in the human body. In addition to muscle and bone, the musculoskeletal system relies on some other tissue types to help its work. Bones are connected to other bones by an elastic tissue called ligaments. The joints, where one bone meets another bone, are covered in a rubbery tissue called cartilage. Muscles are connected to bones by a tough tissue called tendons.

Skin, hair, and nails make up the integumentary system. The name for this system comes from the Latin word *integumentum*, which means "covering." Skin covers the whole body as well as the inside of some of its cavities. The skin has such an important job to do, and comes under so much attack—from bumps, sunlight, water, and chemicals—that it is one of the most regenerative (able to replace itself) parts of the body. The cells in the upper layers of skin, called the epidermis, are constantly being replaced. It takes around a month for the surface to be replaced entirely. Old skin cells are rubbed away, making up around half of household dust.

Head

Neck

Greater trochanter

Lesser trochanter

This image of the stapes was captured by an electron microscope. The stapes helps to pass on sound vibrations inside the ear.

The head of the femur meets the pelvic bone at the hip joint, while the lower end of the femur meets the tibia (shin bone) and patella (kneecap) at the knee joint.

Lateral condyle

Medial condyle

Patellar surface

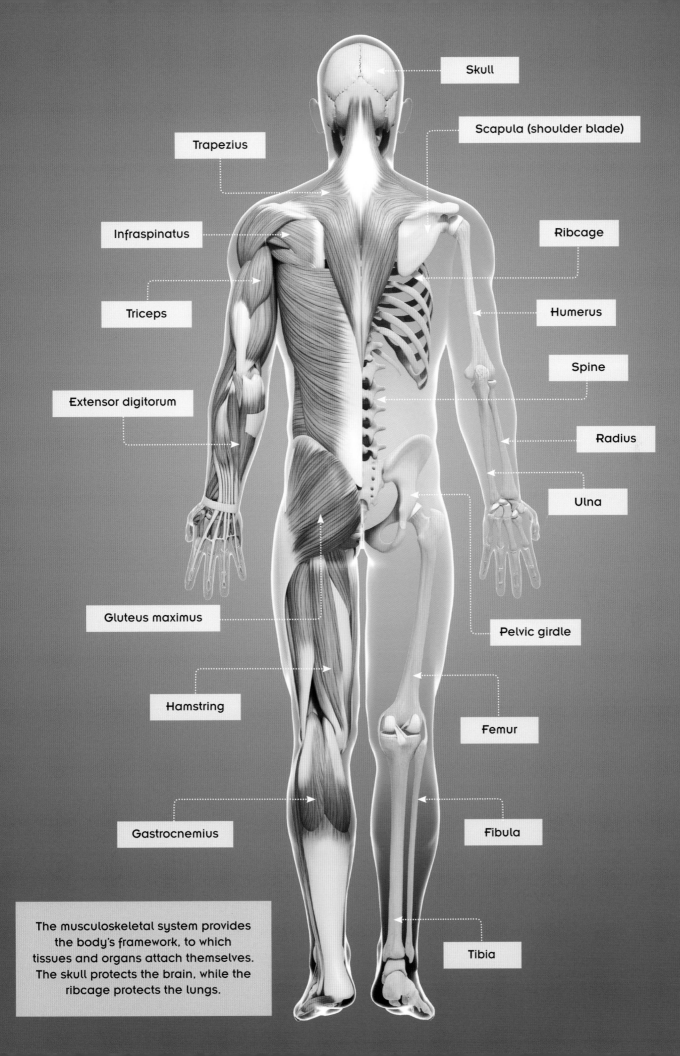

Skull

Scapula (shoulder blade)

Trapezius

Infraspinatus

Ribcage

Triceps

Humerus

Spine

Extensor digitorum

Radius

Ulna

Gluteus maximus

Pelvic girdle

Hamstring

Femur

Gastrocnemius

Fibula

Tibia

The musculoskeletal system provides the body's framework, to which tissues and organs attach themselves. The skull protects the brain, while the ribcage protects the lungs.

BONES

Bones do more than provide structure and protection. At the heart of bones is bone marrow, where blood cells are made. Your bones are also stores of essential minerals, such as calcium, which are released into the blood when needed.

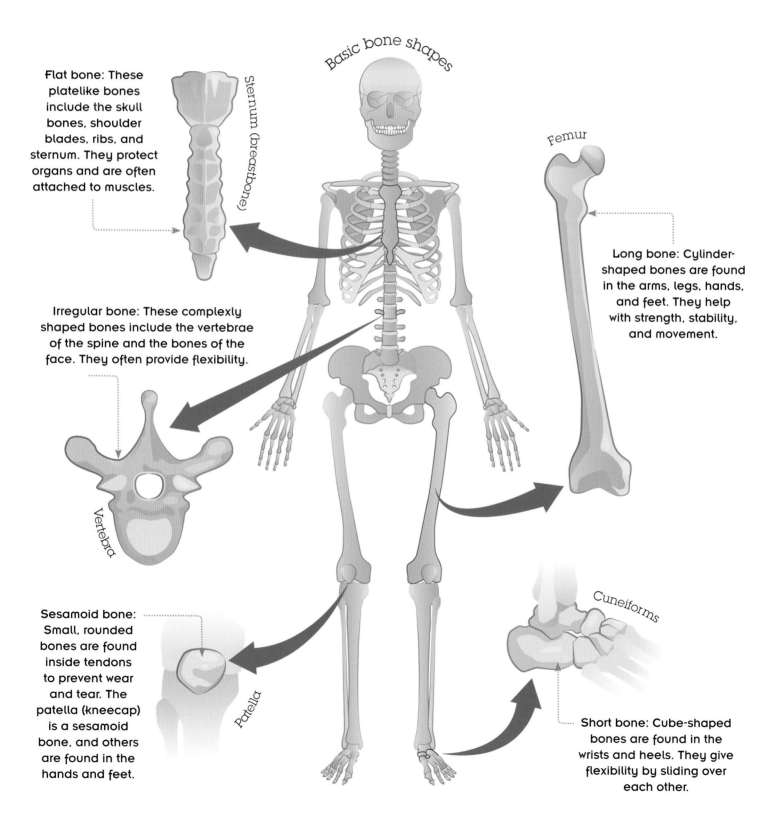

Basic bone shapes

Flat bone: These platelike bones include the skull bones, shoulder blades, ribs, and sternum. They protect organs and are often attached to muscles.

Sternum (breastbone)

Femur

Long bone: Cylinder-shaped bones are found in the arms, legs, hands, and feet. They help with strength, stability, and movement.

Irregular bone: These complexly shaped bones include the vertebrae of the spine and the bones of the face. They often provide flexibility.

Vertebra

Sesamoid bone: Small, rounded bones are found inside tendons to prevent wear and tear. The patella (kneecap) is a sesamoid bone, and others are found in the hands and feet.

Patella

Cuneiforms

Short bone: Cube-shaped bones are found in the wrists and heels. They give flexibility by sliding over each other.

Blood vessels supply the bone cells with oxygen, as well as carrying away new blood cells.

Forming the outer wall of all bones, compact bone is strong and hard.

Spongy bone, found inside many bones, is weaker but more flexible than compact bone, so it absorbs the shock of bumps and bangs.

Inside a bone

Bone is a living tissue made of and by bone cells. Its key ingredients are collagen, a protein that gives a soft framework, and calcium phosphate, a mineral that adds strength.

Bone marrow, found at the heart of most bones, is where blood cells are made.

In an adult's long bones, the epiphyseal line marks the point where the bone used to grow longer during the childhood and teen years.

Skull

The frontal bone is around 7 mm (0.28 in) thick.

Two nasal bones form the upper third of the nose, while the lower third is formed from cartilage.

The parietal bone is marked by two curved lines, where the temporal muscle—which is used for chewing—attaches.

The occipital bone protects the base of the skull.

The upper jaw, called the maxilla, is fixed.

The temporal bone houses the ears.

The only moveable bone in the skull is the lower jaw, called the mandible.

Skeleton

Average adult weight: 9.3 kg (20.5 lb)

Main functions: Enabling movement, providing support and protection, making blood cells, and storing minerals

Body systems: Musculoskeletal, cardiovascular, and immune

Medical breakthrough: In 1939, Wilton M. Krogman wrote a guide to identifying skeletons by the shape of their bones, which can reveal whether the person was male or female and at what age they died. His methods are still used to identify the victims of crimes and to investigate ancient skeletons.

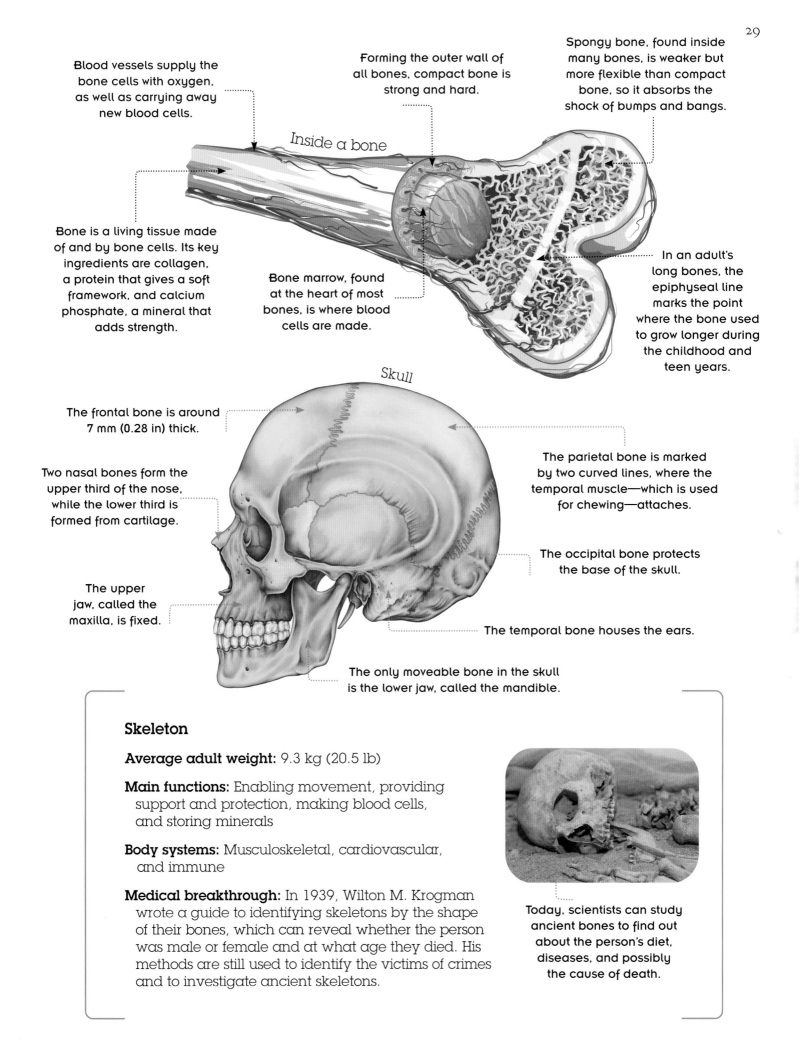

Today, scientists can study ancient bones to find out about the person's diet, diseases, and possibly the cause of death.

LOOKING INSIDE

In 1895, Wilhelm Röntgen created the first image of the inside of the body taken from its exterior: an X-ray of his wife's hand. Today, doctors called radiologists use a wide range of medical imaging devices to diagnose and treat injuries and diseases.

X-rays are an invisible and powerful form of energy. Like visible light (which human eyes can see), X-rays are reflected by some materials and absorbed by others. When the body is placed between an X-ray source and a photographic film, an image forms. Bones absorb X-rays, creating lighter areas on the image. Softer tissue lets X-rays pass through, leaving darker areas on the image. X-rays are often used to examine teeth and broken bones. Since large doses of X-rays can be harmful, both radiologists and patients wear protective clothing.

X-ray images

These X-rays show a fracture in a boy's tibia, in the lower leg.

A computerized tomography (CT) scan uses a series of X-rays taken from different directions. A computer program puts together the images to create cross-sections ("slices") of organs.

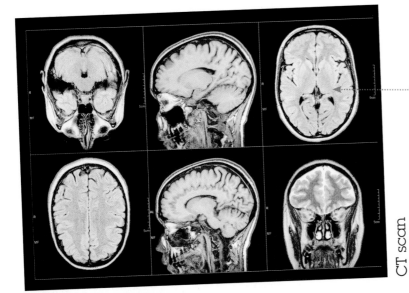

CT scan

CT scans are often used to examine the brain.

For a magnetic resonance imaging (MRI) scan, a patient lies in a large tube that contains powerful magnets. The magnets make tiny particles in the body, called protons, line up in the same direction. Bursts of radio waves, which are an invisible form of energy, knock the protons out of alignment. When the radio waves are turned off, the protons line up again, which sends out radio signals. The protons in different types of tissue line up at different speeds and produce different signals, which creates an image showing organs, tissues, and bones.

MRI scan

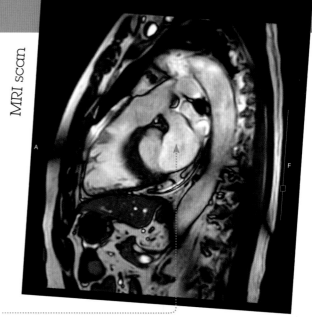

MRI scans can be used to examine almost any part of the body, including the heart.

An ultrasound scan uses sound waves that are too high for the human ear to hear. The sound waves can pass through soft tissue, but bounce off harder tissue, such as muscles and bone.

Ultrasound scan

A moving image, showing "echoes" of the sound waves, is displayed on a screen.

An ultrasound probe gives off very high-pitched sound waves.

Ultrasounds do not damage the body, so they are often used to see an unborn baby in its mother's womb.

JOINTS

Joints are where bones meet other bones. Some joints, known as synovial joints, enable the two bones to move. These joints contain synovial fluid, which helps them move smoothly. Fibrous joints, such as those between most of the skull bones, are fixed. Cartilaginous joints offer a small amount of movement.

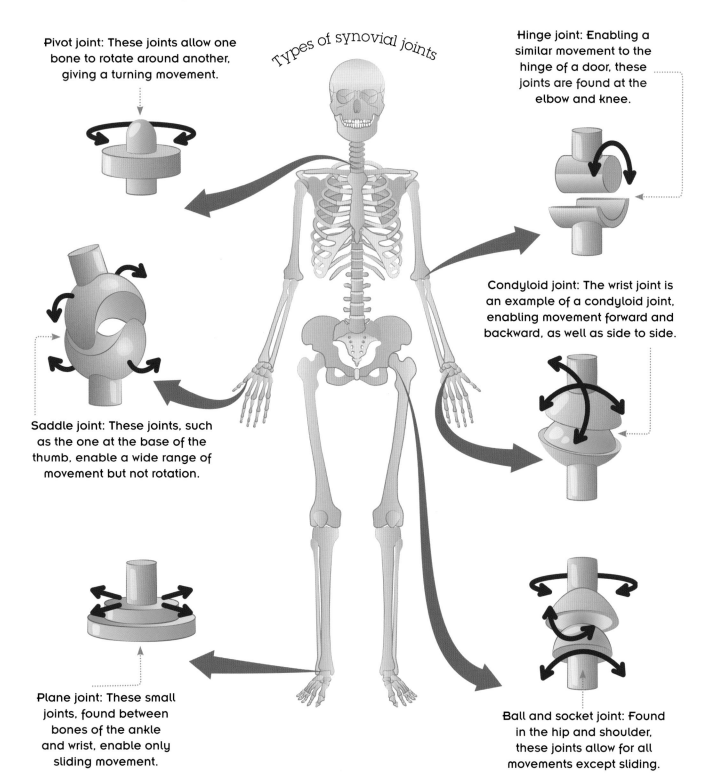

Types of synovial joints

Pivot joint: These joints allow one bone to rotate around another, giving a turning movement.

Hinge joint: Enabling a similar movement to the hinge of a door, these joints are found at the elbow and knee.

Condyloid joint: The wrist joint is an example of a condyloid joint, enabling movement forward and backward, as well as side to side.

Saddle joint: These joints, such as the one at the base of the thumb, enable a wide range of movement but not rotation.

Plane joint: These small joints, found between bones of the ankle and wrist, enable only sliding movement.

Ball and socket joint: Found in the hip and shoulder, these joints allow for all movements except sliding.

Hand

Average adult weight: 0.4 kg (0.9 lb)

Main functions: Grasping, communicating, and touching

Body systems: Musculoskeletal and nervous

Medical breakthrough: The physician Augustin Jacob Landré-Beauvais gave the first full description of rheumatoid arthritis in 1800. This disorder causes swollen and painful joints, particularly in the hands, feet, and spine.

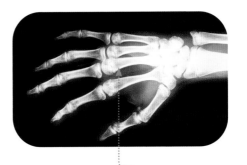

As revealed in this X-ray, each hand is made up of 27 bones and many joints, as well as 34 muscles and over 100 ligaments and tendons.

Fibrous joint

The skull bones are joined by fibrous tissue, which allows for growth during childhood but hardens with age.

Cartilaginous joints

Cartilage joins the ribs to the breastbone, enabling the ribcage to expand a little as you breathe in.

Fibrocartilage, a mixture of cartilage and fibrous tissue, enables slight movement of the vertebrae of the spine, while absorbing the force of bumps.

There are around 360 joints in the human body, letting us move and grow.

Bendy but tough cartilage covers the ends of the bones to help smooth movement.

Synovial joint

Ligaments join together the bones that make a joint, in this case the knee.

Through an electron microscope, you can see tendons (tinted pink) attached to the surface of a bone (tinted green).

MUSCLES

There are three types of muscle: skeletal, heart, and smooth. Skeletal muscle pulls on your bones, so you can run and jump. Unlike skeletal muscle, the other types of muscle work without you thinking about it.

All muscle types are made of cells called myofibers. In skeletal muscle, these cells are long and thin. Packed inside the cells are thousands of myofilaments. It is myofilaments that enable muscles to contract (tighten), as they can overlap and slide over each other—a little like interlocking fingers—making each muscle cell shorter.

Inside each skeletal muscle are bundles of myofibers, wrapped in a connective tissue called fascia. Each muscle is composed of many myofiber bundles. The entire muscle is also wrapped in fascia. At either end of a skeletal muscle are tough cords of fascia, called tendons. Tendons attach to bones and do the work of pulling.

The heart is composed of heart muscle, which contracts, making your heart beat. Smooth muscle is found in the walls of

organs such as those in the digestive system, where it pushes food through from one part to the next. In skeletal muscle, myofibers are parallel to each other. In heart muscle, the myofibers branch out to each other, while in smooth muscle the shorter cells make slow, wavelike movements that enable them to work for long periods without getting tired.

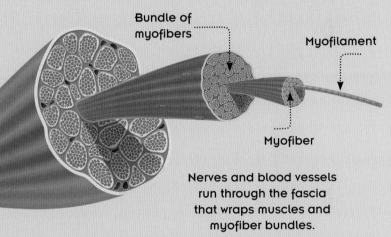

Bundle of myofibers

Myofilament

Myofiber

Nerves and blood vessels run through the fascia that wraps muscles and myofiber bundles.

Skeletal muscle

Sartorius muscle

Average adult length: 47 cm (18 in)

Main functions: Running through the thigh, between the hip and knee, to bend and rotate the femur and knee

Body system: Musculoskeletal

Medical breakthrough: In 1543, Andreas Vesalius was the first to draw and describe all the body's muscles in his series of books, *De Humani Corporis Fabrica Libri Septem* ("On the Fabric of the Human Body in Seven Books").

Vesalius is often called the founder of human anatomy, which is the study of the body and all its parts.

MOVEMENT

Skeletal muscles make all our conscious movements, from running to writing. Muscles can only contract, or shorten, which means a muscle can pull a bone but never push it. This is why skeletal muscles work in pairs, which are able to pull bones in opposite directions.

A movement such as extending then bending the arm involves a pair of muscles: the triceps and biceps. When the triceps contracts, it pulls on the elbow joint, straightening the arm. When the biceps contracts, it pulls the forearm upward.

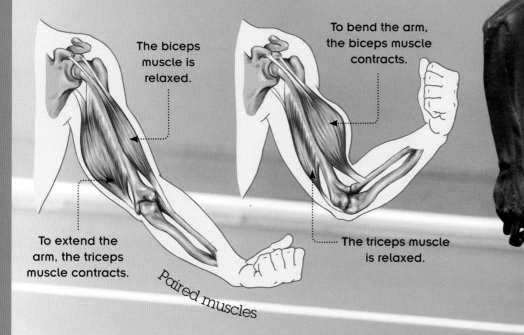

The biceps muscle is relaxed.

To bend the arm, the biceps muscle contracts.

To extend the arm, the triceps muscle contracts.

The triceps muscle is relaxed.

Paired muscles

Exercise can make your skeletal muscles grow bigger and stronger, by increasing the size of the myofibers. Repeatedly performing a muscle contraction, such as lifting a weight with the lower arm, makes the myofibers tear. The body immediately sets to work mending them and growing new myofilaments. In contrast, exercise does not make you grow more heart muscle, but it does make the existing heart muscle stronger.

There are two types of muscle cells: slow twitch and fast twitch. Most muscles contain a mixture of both. Slow-twitch myofibers contract slowly but are also slow to tire. Long-distance runners have a greater quantity of slow-twitch fibers. Fast-twitch myofibers contract quickly but also get tired more quickly. Sprinters, who run short distances very fast, have more of these muscle cells.

Record-breaking sprinter Usain Bolt has many fast-twitch myofibers.

Reflex movement

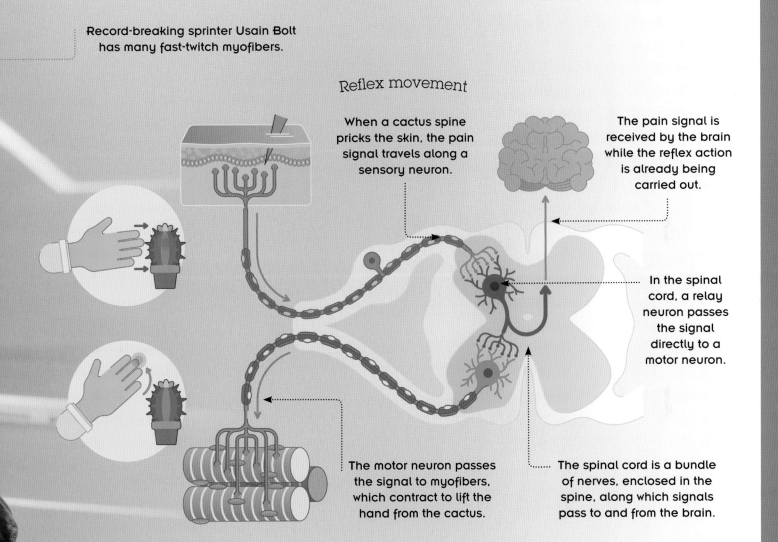

When a cactus spine pricks the skin, the pain signal travels along a sensory neuron.

The pain signal is received by the brain while the reflex action is already being carried out.

In the spinal cord, a relay neuron passes the signal directly to a motor neuron.

The motor neuron passes the signal to myofibers, which contract to lift the hand from the cactus.

The spinal cord is a bundle of nerves, enclosed in the spine, along which signals pass to and from the brain.

Skeletal muscles receive the instruction to contract from the brain. An electrical signal travels from the brain, down the spinal cord, and along a particular type of nerve, called a motor neuron. The signal passes from a motor neuron to myofibers. These signals travel at 70–120 m (230–393 ft) per second. However, the body also has reflexes, which are automatic movements that protect you from harm. These movements are in response to a trigger—such as touching a sharp or hot object—and they bypass the brain so they can happen even faster.

HAIR

The average person has 5 million hairs growing from their skin, with over 100,000 strands on their scalp. Hair has three main purposes: keeping you warm, protecting your head from sunlight, and preventing dust or bacteria entering the eyes, nose, and ears.

The hair shaft has three layers: a spongy core, a middle layer of keratin bundles, and a see-through outer cuticle.

This tiny muscle, called an arrector pilli, can pull on hair to make it stand up straight (see page 45).

A sebaceous gland makes oil, called sebum, that keeps hair and skin lubricated.

The shaft of each hair is made of a tough material called keratin, which is also found in skin and nails.

Hair structure

Each hair is anchored inside a tube of skin called a follicle.

Blood vessels supply the base of each hair with oxygen and nutrients.

Keratin-making cells called keratinocytes divide constantly, making new cells that push old cells upward, creating hair growth. The old cells die as they move away from the base, so the hair strand consists of dead cells.

Hair growth cycle

The anagen phase is the period when a hair is growing, which can last up to 6 years for hairs on the scalp and only weeks for eyebrow hairs, which is why they are much shorter.

After a resting period, known as the telogen phase, a new hair starts to grow, pushing the old hair out.

Hair on the scalp grows around 1.25 cm (0.5 in) every month.

During the catagen phase, the follicle shrinks, making the hair bulb pull away from its source of oxygen and nutrients.

Keratinocyte

Average adult size: 0.0035 cm (0.0014 in) across

Main functions: Forming hair, nails, and skin; and providing a barrier against heat, cold, sunlight, water, water loss, bacteria, fungi, parasites, and viruses

Body system: Integumentary

Medical breakthrough: Since 1982, keratin has been used to make materials for healing wounds, medicines, medical devices, and dentistry.

Under a powerful microscope, you can see hair, covered by its scaly cuticle, growing from follicles in the skin.

Straight hair grows from a follicle that is round.

Curly hair grows from a flattened, oval-shaped follicle.

Hair color and texture

Black hair gets its color from a pigment called eumelanin, while red hair gets its shade from the pigment pheomelanin. Hair between those shades has a mixture of the two pigments.

As we get older, we start producing less pigment, resulting in hair that turns slowly white. Men may also lose hair from their scalp, resulting in baldness, due to hormones that shrink hair follicles.

NAILS

Like hair, nails are made of tough keratin. Nails protect the ends of the fingers and toes, as well as helping to pick things up. Nails grow around 0.5 cm (0.2 in) a month, but fingernails grow a little faster than toenails, perhaps because they experience more wear and tear.

Nails are harder and less flexible than hair because the keratinocyte cells in the nails contain more keratin and are more closely packed. Nail growth takes place in the root, at the base of the nail, beneath the skin of the finger or toe. Here, the keratinocyte cells divide continually, creating new cells that push out the older ones, creating growth. The older cells thicken and die, so the nail you can see is made of dead cells.

The nail body, which lies flat on the skin of the nail bed, appears pinkish because it is quite transparent, letting you see blood vessels in the skin below. The tip of the nail, where it grows beyond the edge of the finger or toe, is thick and opaque (difficult to see through).

At the base of each nail is a whiter, half-moon-shaped area called the lunula. The

lunula is sometimes wholly or partly hidden by the cuticle, a thickened layer of skin that grows over the junction between the nail and skin to protect it from bacteria. The lunula appears whiter than the rest of the nail because of a thicker layer of skin beneath, blocking out the blood vessels below.

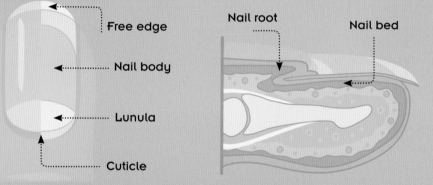

There are no nerves in nails, so you cannot feel them being cut. However, if a nail rips or is cut too short, the nerves in the skin below are exposed, making it feel particularly sensitive to touch and pain.

Fingernail

Average adult weight: 1 g (0.04 oz)

Main functions: Protecting and strengthening the fingertips; and scratching, separating, and picking up

Body system: Integumentary

Medical breakthrough: Nail growth can reveal information about our health. In 2021, doctors noticed that people who had suffered from COVID-19 also often had a horizontal groove across their nails, resulting from nail growth being disrupted.

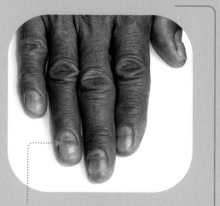

A deep horizontal groove across a fingernail, called a Beau's line, can be the result of illness.

Fingernails make it easier to perform delicate hand movements, which are needed when we play "pick-up sticks."

Ridges on the epidermis of the fingertips help with gripping, by making the fingertips rougher, and with feeling texture. The ridges form patterns unique to each person, which are transferred to touched surfaces by sweat and oil. In the event of a crime, police officers can use chemicals to reveal fingerprints then use them for identification.

SKIN

Your skin is in three layers: the outer epidermis; the middle dermis, which is loaded with blood vessels and nerves; and the bottom hypodermis, which is partly made of fat and connects your skin to your muscles and bones.

In a healthy adult, around half of the hypodermis is made up of fat. This fat helps to keep you warm, protects you from bumps, and stores some of the energy you take in from food.

The middle layer of skin, the dermis, contains strong fibers that make the skin slightly elastic, enabling it to stretch as you move. As we get older, these fibers weaken, causing wrinkles. The blood vessels of the dermis feed the bottom layer of cells in the epidermis. In addition, sensory receptors in the dermis respond to touch, temperature, and pain, then send signals to the brain along nerves.

The epidermis itself has five layers. The bottom layer contains living keratinocytes. These cells divide, creating new keratinocytes that are pushed upward. As the cells rise, they produce keratin, which makes the epidermis tough and waterproof. The rising cells

also start to flatten and die, so the upper layer of skin is made only of dead cells.

Cells called melanocytes also live in the bottom layer of the epidermis. They produce the pigment melanin, which makes surrounding keratinocytes darker. The more active our melanocytes, the darker our skin. Melanocyte activity is programmed by our genes, which are passed down from our parents. Melanocytes also become more active when skin is exposed to sunlight.

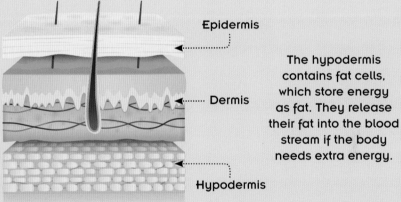

Epidermis

Dermis

Hypodermis

The hypodermis contains fat cells, which store energy as fat. They release their fat into the blood stream if the body needs extra energy.

Melanocyte

Average adult size: 0.0007 cm (0.0003 in) across

Main functions: Making the pigment melanin, which darkens the skin to protect it from the Sun's harmful ultraviolet rays; and capturing disease-causing invaders that try to enter through the skin

Body systems: Integumentary and immune

Medical breakthrough: If skin, particularly pale skin, is exposed to too much ultraviolet light, melanocytes can become cancerous, causing a growth called melanoma that usually affects pigmented patches called moles. The Scottish surgeon John Hunter performed the first operation to remove a melanoma in 1787.

You can reduce your risk of melanoma by applying sunscreen, covering skin with clothing and a hat, wearing good-quality sunglasses, and staying in the shade.

TEMPERATURE

When you are healthy, your body temperature ranges from around 36.1 °C (97 °F) to 37.2 °C (99 °F). At this temperature, your body's cells and organs can carry out their work well. The body goes to great lengths to keep itself at the right temperature.

Your body heat comes from the movement of your skeletal muscles and the work of your cells, which constantly release heat as they generate energy. Part of the brain called the hypothalamus (see page 100) watches over body temperature and starts mechanisms to raise or lower it when necessary. If the body gets extremely cold, making its temperature fall to less than 32° C (89.6 °F), a condition called hypothermia may set in, resulting in a slowdown of the body's functions. If a person gets very hot, making their body temperature rise above 40 °C (104 °F) for a long period, their cells and organs may struggle to function. Viruses and infections can cause a fever, raising body temperature above 38 °C (100.4 °F). Fever is caused by the hypothalamus raising body temperature to kill off the invader.

A sudden dive into icy water makes the hypothalamus send signals to increase the speed of body processes, which generates more heat.

Eccrine sweat glands are found across most of the body, particularly the forehead, neck, and back. They produce sweat that is mostly water, salts, and waste.

Types of sweat glands

An apocrine sweat gland releases its sweat into a hair follicle.

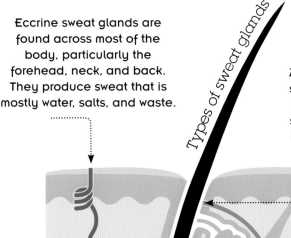

When your body gets hot, during exercise or in hot weather, your hypothalamus sends signals to make you sweat. There are around 3 million sweat glands in your skin, which produce sweat. Once sweat is on the skin surface, it evaporates, which means it turns to gas. The energy needed to make this change is taken from your body heat, cooling you down. On a hot day, you may lose up to 7 liters (4 pints) of sweat, which is why it is important to drink plenty of water. In addition, blood vessels leading to the skin are relaxed, letting more blood flow through the skin and more heat to be lost.

Apocrine sweat glands are in parts of the body that are hairy when we are adults, such as the armpits and groin. After puberty, these glands produce thicker sweat that has a strong smell, produced by bacteria on the skin breaking down the sweat's proteins and fats.

If you get cold, you will start to shiver. Skeletal muscles make small shaking movements, creating warmth as they use energy. Tiny muscles (see page 38) at the base of hairs (everywhere on the body apart from the face) pull hairs upright. This results in little bumps on the skin, called goosebumps. This reaction to cold was much more useful to our hairy, ape ancestors, as it made their thick hair trap a layer of air next to the skin, which slowed heat loss. The hypothalamus also signals blood vessels leading to the skin to contract, letting less blood flow through the skin and lose heat. In extreme cold, this reaction can result in pale or numb fingers and toes.

Goosebumps can appear when you are cold, frightened, or tickled.

Chapter 3

LUNGS, HEART, AND BLOOD

Your lungs and heart work together to carry life-sustaining oxygen to every part of the body. The lungs are responsible for breathing, which gives oxygen to your blood. The heart pumps blood through a network of tubes called blood vessels, which stretches for an extraordinary 95,000 km (60,000 miles).

The lungs and airways form the respiratory system. This body system's key role is gas exchange. This is when oxygen is passed to the blood; and waste carbon dioxide is taken from the blood. Oxygen is needed as fuel by every cell in the body so it can break up glucose sugar (from the food you eat) to make the energy it needs. As a cell carries out this process, it also makes carbon dioxide as a waste product. This waste is passed to the blood, which carries it to the lungs, so it can be breathed out.

The heart, blood vessels, and blood form the cardiovascular system. As your heart beats, it pumps blood through blood vessels that range in size from the aorta, around 2 cm (0.8 in) wide, to tiny capillaries, which have one-cell-thick walls that let oxygen and carbon dioxide pass through to tissues and organs.

The average 11-year-old has around 2.6 liters (0.7 gallons) of blood. More than half (55 percent) of blood is a yellowish liquid called plasma, which is largely water. Plasma carries nutrients from food; messengers called hormones; proteins needed around the body; carbon dioxide and other waste; and trillions of blood cells. The three types of blood cells are red blood cells, white blood cells, and platelets. Red blood cells make up 44 percent of blood, while white blood cells and platelets fill the remaining 1 percent.

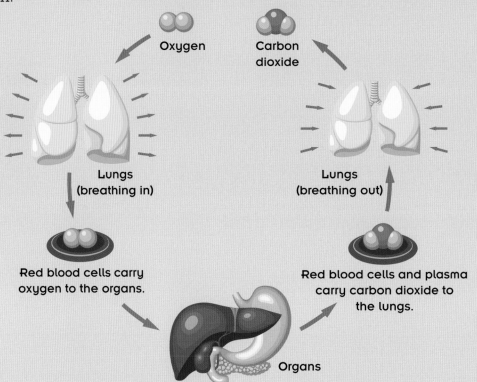

Oxygen

Carbon dioxide

Lungs (breathing in)

Lungs (breathing out)

Every minute, around 300 ml (10 fl oz) of oxygen is passed from the lungs to the blood.

Red blood cells carry oxygen to the organs.

Red blood cells and plasma carry carbon dioxide to the lungs.

Organs

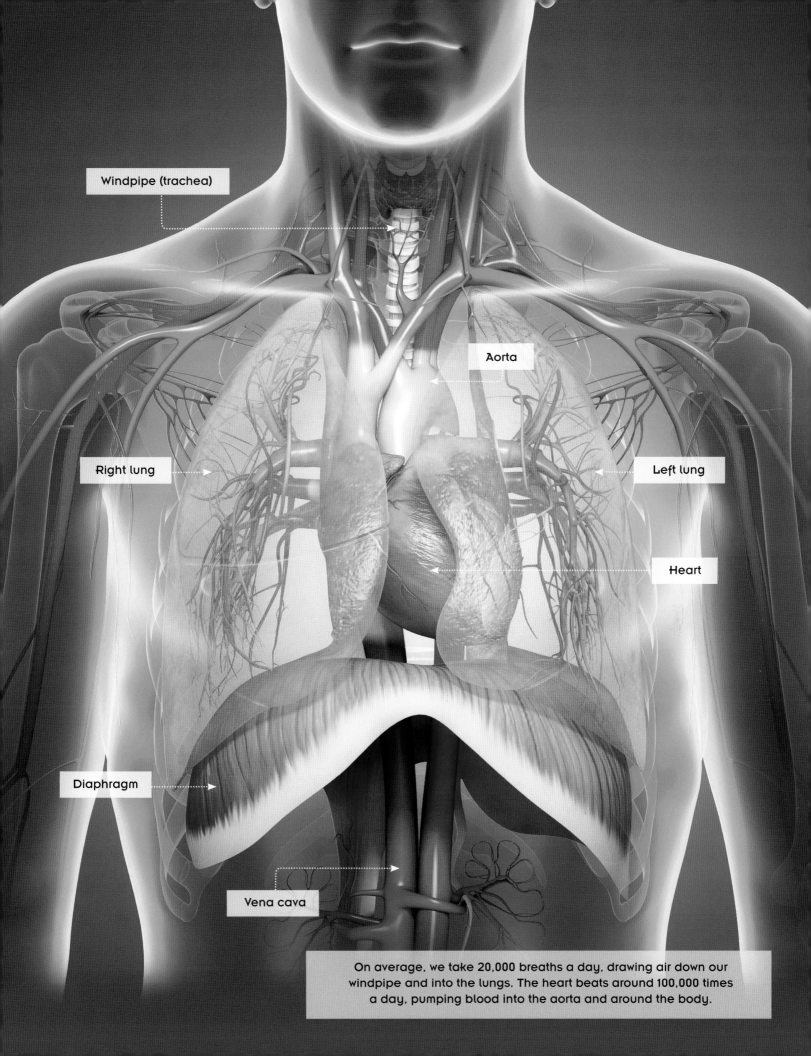

Windpipe (trachea)

Aorta

Right lung

Left lung

Heart

Diaphragm

Vena cava

On average, we take 20,000 breaths a day, drawing air down our windpipe and into the lungs. The heart beats around 100,000 times a day, pumping blood into the aorta and around the body.

This X-ray of the right lung shows the bronchus branching into narrower and narrower airways. The right lung is slightly bigger than the left lung, which has to fit around the heart.

LUNGS

Every moment of every day, your lungs are doing two essential jobs. The first is taking oxygen gas from the air you breathe—and transferring it to the blood. The second is releasing a waste gas, carbon dioxide, from the blood into the air.

We are able to breathe because of the diaphragm, a sheet of muscle just below the lungs. When we breathe in (inhale), the diaphragm flattens, creating more room in the chest so the lungs expand. Air rushes in—through the nose or mouth—to fill the space in the lungs. When we breathe out (exhale), the diaphragm relaxes, pushing air out of the lungs.

After air enters the nose or mouth, it travels through the throat, into a tube called the windpipe (or trachea). Where the windpipe meets the lungs, it branches into two, one tube traveling into the left lung and one into the right. Each of these tubes is called a bronchus (plural "bronchi"). Each bronchus divides again and again, into narrower and narrower airways. From these airways, air flows into tiny baglike structures called alveoli. This is where gas exchange happens.

The alveoli have very thin walls that oxygen can pass through into the blood. The alveoli also soak up carbon dioxide from the blood. When we breathe out, carbon dioxide flows up through the windpipe and out of the nose or mouth. Our breath also contains some unused oxygen and nitrogen, which is a gas in air that we do not need.

Air travels in and out.

The lungs contain up to 500 million alveoli, each one around 0.2 mm (0.008 in) across.

Alveolus (plural "alvioli")

Capillary

Oxygen passes into the blood running through a capillary.

Carbon dioxide is soaked up.

Lungs

Average adult weight: 1.3 kg (2.9 lb)

Main functions: Gas exchange, filtering small clots from the blood, and helping speech as air travels from the lungs through the voice box (see page 122)

Body system: Respiratory

Medical breakthrough: In 1661, while studying frog lungs under a microscope, Italian physician Marcello Malpighi was the first to discover alveoli and the network of capillaries that surrounds them.

Marcello Malpighi noticed that frogs and dogs have similar lungs to humans, but insects do not.

HEART

Around the size of your fist, your heart is positioned just to the left side of your chest. It is a muscular pump that squeezes blood carrying oxygen and nutrients to the rest of the body, as well as pushing blood carrying carbon dioxide to the lungs. The heart has four chambers: the left atrium and ventricle, and the right atrium and ventricle.

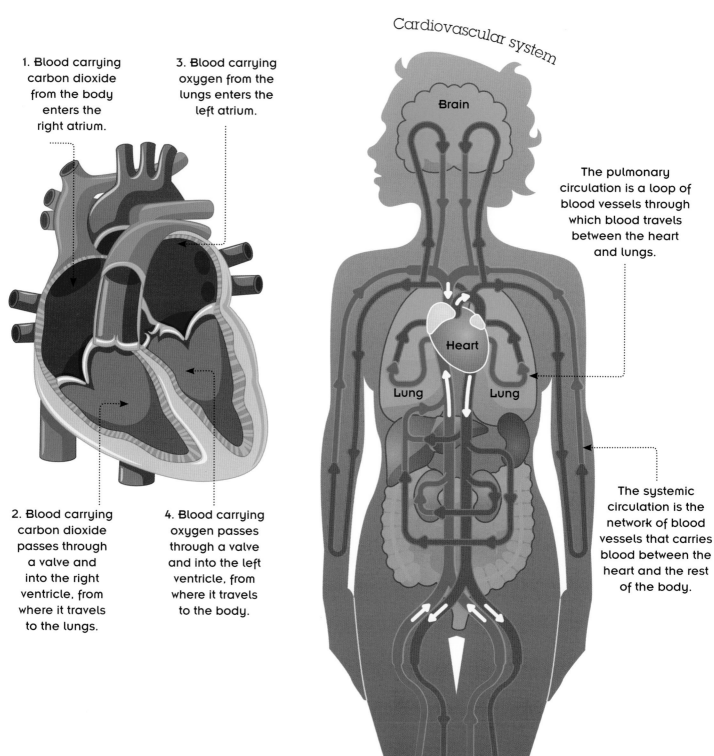

Chambers of the heart

1. Blood carrying carbon dioxide from the body enters the right atrium.

3. Blood carrying oxygen from the lungs enters the left atrium.

2. Blood carrying carbon dioxide passes through a valve and into the right ventricle, from where it travels to the lungs.

4. Blood carrying oxygen passes through a valve and into the left ventricle, from where it travels to the body.

Cardiovascular system

Brain

Heart

Lung   Lung

The pulmonary circulation is a loop of blood vessels through which blood travels between the heart and lungs.

The systemic circulation is the network of blood vessels that carries blood between the heart and the rest of the body.

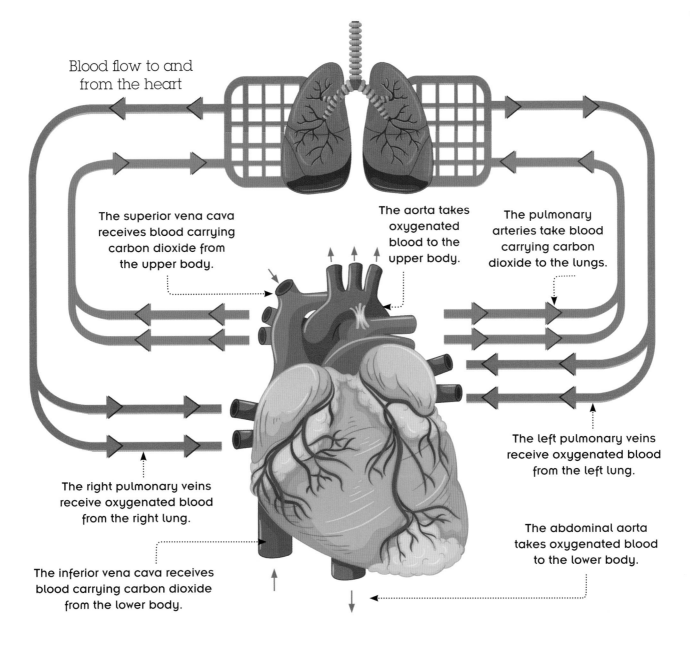

Blood flow to and from the heart

The superior vena cava receives blood carrying carbon dioxide from the upper body.

The aorta takes oxygenated blood to the upper body.

The pulmonary arteries take blood carrying carbon dioxide to the lungs.

The left pulmonary veins receive oxygenated blood from the left lung.

The right pulmonary veins receive oxygenated blood from the right lung.

The abdominal aorta takes oxygenated blood to the lower body.

The inferior vena cava receives blood carrying carbon dioxide from the lower body.

Heart

Average adult weight: 300 g (10 oz)

Main functions: Pumping oxygen-rich blood and other vital materials to the rest of the body, and receiving deoxygenated blood from the body then sending it to the lungs

Body system: Cardiovascular

Medical breakthrough: In 1967, surgeon Christiaan Barnard performed the first human heart transplant on a patient whose heart was failing. Louis Washkansky was given the heart of somebody who had just died.

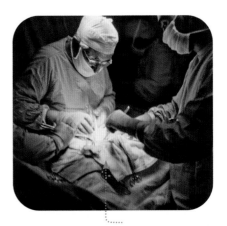

Since Barnard (above left) performed the first heart transplant, more than 50,000 people have been given new hearts.

TAKING EXERCISE

When you run, dance, or play a sport, your busy muscles need more oxygen to fuel their work. The lungs and heart have to work harder, so you take more breaths per minute and your heart beats more frequently. Regular exercise makes the heart and lungs stronger.

To meet your muscles' extra need for oxygen, your breathing has to increase from about 15–30 times per minute when resting, up to about 40–60 times per minute during exercise. When not exercising, an adult's heart beats 60 to 100 times per minute. When exercising, the average adult's heart can beat 175 times per minute. The average 11-year-old's heart beats around 130 times per minute during exercise. The number of heart beats per minute, known as heart rate, can be checked by taking the pulse on your wrist. The beats can be felt as blood surges through the wrist's radial artery.

Hold out one of your hands, with your palm facing upward.

Taking the pulse

Regular exercise makes the heart and lungs more efficient at getting oxygen into the blood and transporting it to the muscles.

Gently press the first finger and middle finger of your other hand on the inside of your wrist, at the base of your thumb. Count how many times you feel the heart beat in 1 minute.

Regular exercise makes the muscles more efficient, so they need less oxygen to do their work.

If you run
frequently,
you will
become less
breathless
over time.

When not exercising hard, cells use a process called aerobic respiration (meaning "producing energy using oxygen") to release energy from glucose. The waste products of aerobic respiration are carbon dioxide and water. However, if muscle cells cannot get enough oxygen during heavy exercise, they produce energy using a different method, called anaerobic respiration. This method, which can only be used for a short period, produces energy from glucose without using oxygen. It has a different waste product: lactic acid. This acid is responsible for the burning feeling in your muscles during extreme exercise, but the burning fades harmlessly within a few minutes if you rest.

Aerobic respiration

Oxygen

Glucose

Carbon dioxide
and water

Energy

In every cell, aerobic respiration takes place in parts called mitochondria.

BLOOD VESSELS

There are three main types of blood vessels: arteries, which carry blood away from the heart; veins, which carry blood to the heart; and capillaries. Tiny, thin-walled capillaries carry blood between veins and arteries while enabling materials to be exchanged between the blood and all the body's tissues.

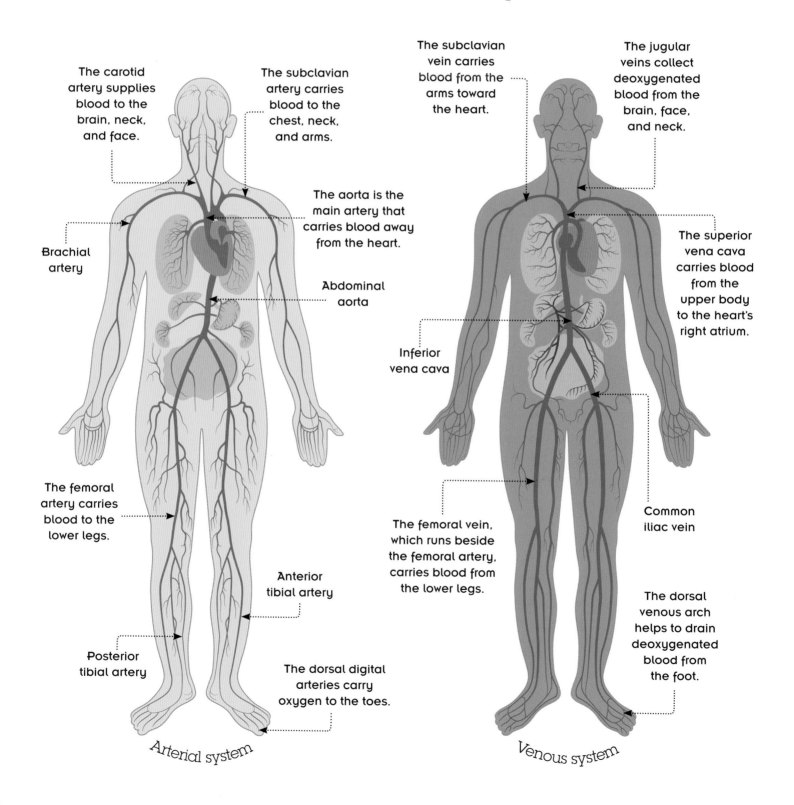

The carotid artery supplies blood to the brain, neck, and face.

The subclavian artery carries blood to the chest, neck, and arms.

The aorta is the main artery that carries blood away from the heart.

Brachial artery

Abdominal aorta

The femoral artery carries blood to the lower legs.

Anterior tibial artery

Posterior tibial artery

The dorsal digital arteries carry oxygen to the toes.

Arterial system

The subclavian vein carries blood from the arms toward the heart.

The jugular veins collect deoxygenated blood from the brain, face, and neck.

The superior vena cava carries blood from the upper body to the heart's right atrium.

Inferior vena cava

The femoral vein, which runs beside the femoral artery, carries blood from the lower legs.

Common iliac vein

The dorsal venous arch helps to drain deoxygenated blood from the foot.

Venous system

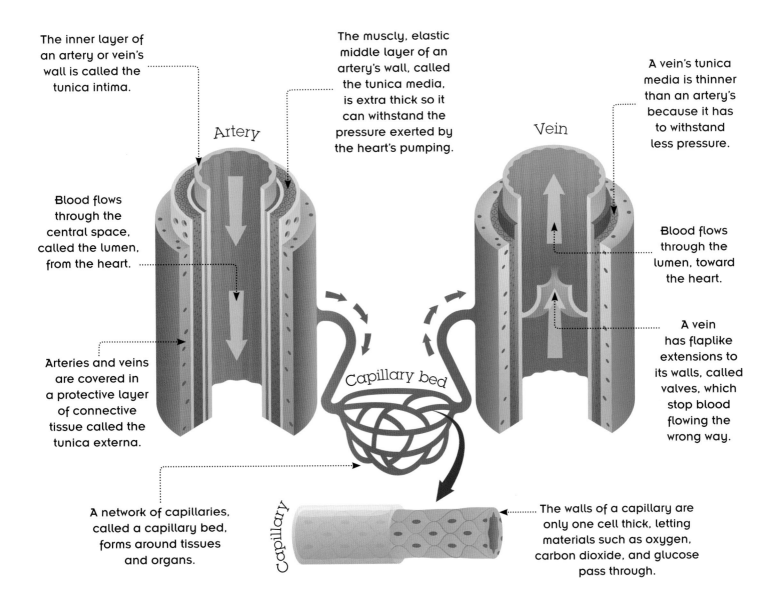

The inner layer of an artery or vein's wall is called the tunica intima.

The muscly, elastic middle layer of an artery's wall, called the tunica media, is extra thick so it can withstand the pressure exerted by the heart's pumping.

A vein's tunica media is thinner than an artery's because it has to withstand less pressure.

Artery

Vein

Blood flows through the central space, called the lumen, from the heart.

Blood flows through the lumen, toward the heart.

Arteries and veins are covered in a protective layer of connective tissue called the tunica externa.

Capillary bed

A vein has flaplike extensions to its walls, called valves, which stop blood flowing the wrong way.

A network of capillaries, called a capillary bed, forms around tissues and organs.

Capillary

The walls of a capillary are only one cell thick, letting materials such as oxygen, carbon dioxide, and glucose pass through.

Blood

Average adult weight: 4.3 kg (9.5 lb)

Main functions: Transporting oxygen and nutrients to the organs and tissues; carrying cells and antibodies that fight infection; transporting waste products to the lungs, kidneys, and liver; and regulating body temperature

Body systems: Cardiovascular, digestive, endocrine, and immune

Medical breakthrough: In 1980, Robert F. Furchgott discovered the mechanism that enables blood vessels leading to the skin capillaries to relax when a person gets hot. This lets more blood flow through the skin and more heat to be lost to the environment.

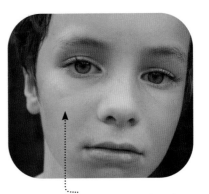

When we get hot, our cheeks flush as more blood flows through the capillaries in the skin.

This image, created using an electron microscope, shows red blood cells (red), white blood cells called lymphocytes (green), and platelets (blue). The cells have been tinted to make them clearer.

RED BLOOD CELLS

There are 20 to 30 *trillion* red blood cells in the average adult's blood. A red blood cell is disk-shaped, with a dip on each side, which increases its surface area so it can exchange as much gas as possible.

Each red blood cell is packed with around 270 million molecules of a substance called hemoglobin. Hemoglobin is red, which is why blood looks red. Hemoglobin contains iron, which binds to oxygen. This is how red blood cells can transport oxygen from the lungs to wherever it is needed. When a red blood cell reaches tissue in need of oxygen, the hemoglobin releases its oxygen.

Around one quarter of the waste carbon dioxide made by cells is also able to bind to red blood cells, which carry it to the lungs. The rest of the waste carbon dioxide travels to the lungs in the plasma.

Red blood cells are made inside bones, in the bone marrow. Around 2 million new ones are made every second. This constant production is

necessary because a red blood cell lives for only around 120 days. When a red blood cell is worn out, it is broken down by white blood cells, then recycled. The heme portion of the hemoglobin is recycled by the liver, becoming an ingredient in bile (see page 74), which helps to break down fats in the intestines. Much of the rest is recycled into new red blood cells.

Red blood cell

Around 70 percent of cells in the whole body are red blood cells.

Oxygen passes into the blood from alveoli.

Oxygen binds to hemoglobin.

Oxygen is released to cells.

Red blood cell

Average size: 0.00078 cm (0.0003 in) across

Main functions: Carrying oxygen from lungs to cells, and carrying carbon dioxide from cells to lungs

Body system: Cardiovascular

Medical breakthrough: In 1900, Austrian doctor Karl Landsteiner discovered that there are different blood types. These types are in part determined by antigens (substances that can trigger the immune system to fight against them) on the surface of red blood cells: antigen A (type A), antigen B (type B), both antigen A and B (type AB), and neither antigen (type O).

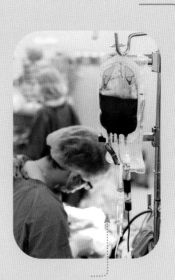

For a blood transfusion, the donated blood must belong to the same blood group as the patient, or their immune system will attack the new blood cells.

UNDER ATTACK

Your body is constantly under attack from invaders too small to see. These invaders include viruses, bacteria, and fungi, as well as other specks of foreign matter, such as chemicals. It is the job of the body's immune system to defend you.

An antigen is any substance that makes our immune system respond, by launching a counter-attack. The immune system's aim is to recognize and destroy antigens. Antigens include tiny living things called viruses, bacteria, and fungi, which can cause disease if they get a foothold in the body. Viruses are the smallest of these invaders, as tiny as 0.000002 cm (0.00000079 in) across. While a healthy immune system can defend itself against most invaders, today our bodies also have help from medications and vaccines (see page 84).

A person can become infected with COVID-19 by breathing in small particles containing the virus SARS-CoV-2. Once inside the body, the virus may cause no symptoms or can cause mild to severe disease, with symptoms including fever, cough, headache, and breathing difficulties.

Your body is laden, both inside and out, with trillions of harmless or even helpful bacteria, but a few can cause disease.

There are millions of different viruses, which can reproduce only inside the cells of another living thing. This can kill or damage cells, causing disease.

SARS-CoV-2 virus

If *Streptococcus pneumoniae* bacteria enter alveoli in the lungs, they can cause a disease called pneumonia, which results in coughing, chest pain, and fever.

Streptococcus pneumoniae bacteria

Of at least 2 million different fungi, only around 300 can cause disease, if they land on the skin or are breathed in.

Microsporum fungi

If *Microsporum* fungi invade skin cells on the feet, they can cause the common disease athlete's foot, which results in itching and flaking skin.

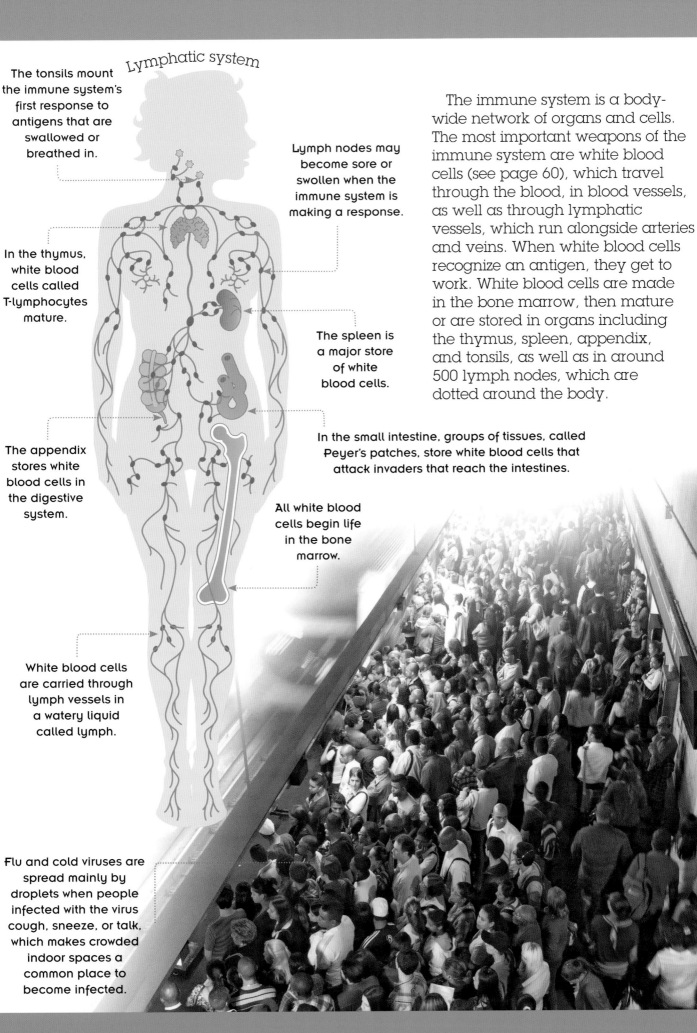

Lymphatic system

The tonsils mount the immune system's first response to antigens that are swallowed or breathed in.

Lymph nodes may become sore or swollen when the immune system is making a response.

In the thymus, white blood cells called T-lymphocytes mature.

The spleen is a major store of white blood cells.

The appendix stores white blood cells in the digestive system.

In the small intestine, groups of tissues, called Peyer's patches, store white blood cells that attack invaders that reach the intestines.

All white blood cells begin life in the bone marrow.

White blood cells are carried through lymph vessels in a watery liquid called lymph.

Flu and cold viruses are spread mainly by droplets when people infected with the virus cough, sneeze, or talk, which makes crowded indoor spaces a common place to become infected.

The immune system is a body-wide network of organs and cells. The most important weapons of the immune system are white blood cells (see page 60), which travel through the blood, in blood vessels, as well as through lymphatic vessels, which run alongside arteries and veins. When white blood cells recognize an antigen, they get to work. White blood cells are made in the bone marrow, then mature or are stored in organs including the thymus, spleen, appendix, and tonsils, as well as in around 500 lymph nodes, which are dotted around the body.

WHITE BLOOD CELLS

The immune system depends on white blood cells to target and destroy invaders. A healthy adult produces around 100 billion white blood cells every day. There are five main types of white blood cells, each with different jobs and abilities: neutrophils, basophils, eosinophils, monocytes, and lymphocytes. There are three main types of lymphocytes: T cells, B cells, and natural killers.

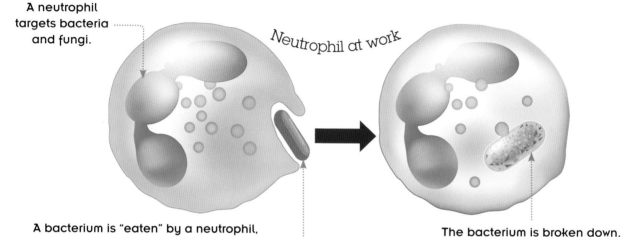

A neutrophil targets bacteria and fungi.

Neutrophil at work

A bacterium is "eaten" by a neutrophil, in a process called phagocytosis.

The bacterium is broken down.

Histamine released by basophils causes cells in the nose to make mucus, which can cause irritation and make you sneeze.

Basophil

A basophil releases a chemical called histamine, which widens blood vessels to increase the flow of blood (and white blood cells) to injured tissue, causing swelling.

An eosinophil targets parasites, such as tiny single-celled amebas, that try to live inside the body.

Eosinophil

A basophil also sends signals to other white blood cells.

Granules hold substances that can destroy invaders.

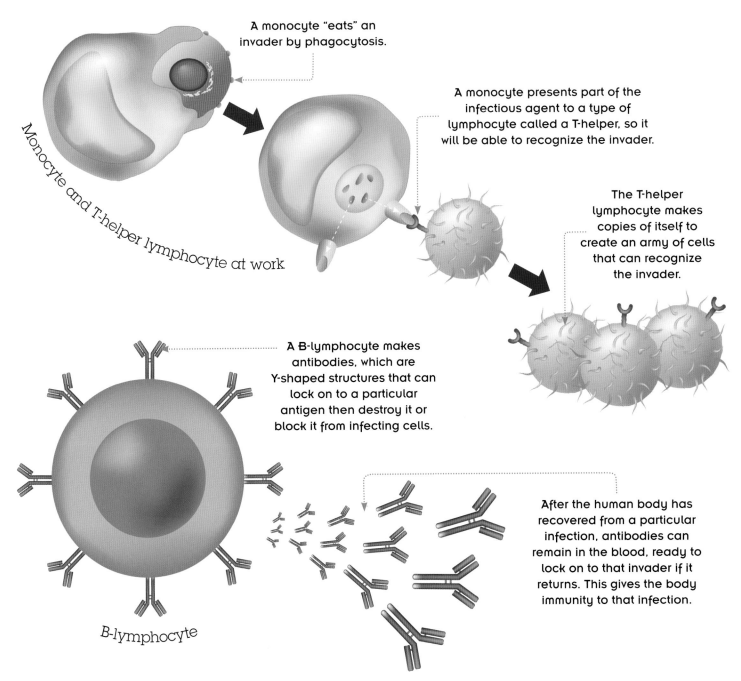

A monocyte "eats" an invader by phagocytosis.

A monocyte presents part of the infectious agent to a type of lymphocyte called a T-helper, so it will be able to recognize the invader.

Monocyte and T-helper lymphocyte at work

The T-helper lymphocyte makes copies of itself to create an army of cells that can recognize the invader.

A B-lymphocyte makes antibodies, which are Y-shaped structures that can lock on to a particular antigen then destroy it or block it from infecting cells.

After the human body has recovered from a particular infection, antibodies can remain in the blood, ready to lock on to that invader if it returns. This gives the body immunity to that infection.

B-lymphocyte

Natural killer lymphocyte

Average size: 0.00065 cm (0.00026 in) across

Main functions: Recognizing cancerous cells and cells infected with viruses, and killing those cells by releasing chemicals called cytokines

Body system: Immune

Medical breakthrough: In 2018, doctors began to run trials on a new treatment for cancer, in which laboratory-engineered natural killer cells are given to patients. Cancer is a disease where cells in a particular part of the body grow and reproduce uncontrollably.

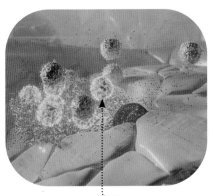

In this illustration, natural killer cells are targeting cancerous cells.

PLATELETS

If you injure yourself, break a blood vessel, and start to bleed, platelets go to work. Within 20 seconds, they begin to clump together to stop the bleeding. Platelets are plate-shaped fragments of bone marrow cells.

Platelets are produced from very large bone marrow cells called megakaryocytes. The megakaryocytes break apart, releasing over a thousand platelets from each megakaryocyte. A healthy adult produces around a trillion platelets every day, which circulate constantly in the blood.

When a blood vessel is broken, platelets are attracted to the rough, torn wall. The platelets start to become sticky, binding to breaks in the wall and to each other. Now the platelets change shape, becoming a ball with long tentacles that can reach out to the broken wall and each other. The platelets also send out chemical signals that attract other platelets to the site. Finally, the platelets team up with a substance in plasma, called

fibrinogen, to make fibrin, which forms a mesh of threads. The mesh traps blood cells and creates a plug. As the plug dries, it hardens into a clot we call a scab.

Although the platelets' job is done, the process of healing continues as new cells are made to replace the broken blood vessel. White blood cells destroy infectious agents around the wound. At last, the clot dissolves as the fibrin is broken down by enzymes, which are substances that bind to molecules and alter them.

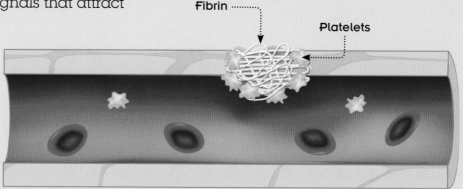

Fibrin ⋯⋯⋯
Platelets

After a minor injury to a blood vessel, it takes no more than a few minutes for a clot to be complete.

Platelet

Average size: 0.00025 cm (0.000098 in) across

Main functions: Stopping bleeding, and protecting from infection by binding and destroying infectious agents

Body systems: Cardiovascular and immune

Medical breakthrough: In 2016, scientists at the University of Cambridge were able to grow megakaryocytes, which produced a few of their own platelets. In the future, laboratory-made platelets could help to stop patients bleeding from severe wounds.

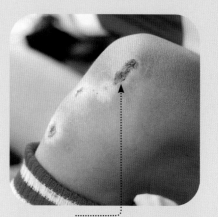

A small scab will normally fall off within a week, after the blood vessels and skin underneath have healed.

In this electron microscope image, we can see a clot formed by joined platelets, which have trapped many red blood cells.

ALLERGIES

Not all foreign substances that enter the body are harmful. Sometimes, the immune system overreacts to a harmless invader, known as an allergen, such as pollen or particular foods. This overreaction is called an allergic reaction.

People may be born with an allergy to a particular substance or they may develop one due to factors in their environment that make their immune system oversensitive, such as air pollution from cars. The first step in an allergic reaction is when the allergen enters the body—through the nose, mouth, or eyes—or, in some cases, touches the skin.

Peanuts

Common food allergies include peanuts, milk, eggs, wheat, soy, and shellfish.

Some people react to breathing in the droppings of dust mites, relatives of spiders just 0.2 mm (0.008 in) long, which live among house dust.

In many countries, more than 1 out of every 100 children are allergic to peanuts.

House dust mite

Pet

It is twice as common to be allergic to cat allergens as to dog allergens.

As soon as the immune system recognizes the allergen, white blood cells release histamine. This chemical causes many of the symptoms of an allergic reaction: swelling, itchy skin, red eyes, and a runny nose. People who suffer from asthma may have difficulty breathing. Asthma is a common lung condition that causes swelling of the airways. In rare cases, an allergic reaction is so severe that it causes anaphylaxis. This is a dangerous condition as it affects heartbeat and constricts the airways.

Tiny grains of pollen are produced by the male parts of flowering plants, then carried to other plants—usually by wind or insects—so they can produce seeds.

Pollen

An allergic reaction can be eased with an antihistamine medication, which stops the body responding to histamine. Anaphylaxis can be treated with an immediate injection of adrenaline, which opens the airways and maintains heartbeat. Specialist doctors can treat some allergies, such as hay fever and insect bites, using allergen immunotherapy, which gradually exposes people to larger amounts of the allergen.

One of the most common allergies is to plant pollen, which can cause a condition called hay fever when breathed in.

Female mosquitoes suck blood through their tubelike mouthparts, after injecting saliva that stops blood from clotting.

Insects that can provoke an allergic reaction with their bites or stings include mosquitoes, bees, and wasps.

If someone has had a severe allergic reaction in the past, they can carry an autoinjector, which they use to deliver a dose of adrenaline if they are exposed to an allergen.

Female mosquito

Some people are allergic to mosquito saliva.

Dead flakes of skin shed by cats can cause an allergic reaction after landing on the lining of the nose or eyes.

Adrenaline autoinjector

Chapter 4

EATING FOR ENERGY

Your digestive system has the task of breaking down the food you eat, stripping it to its basic parts, called nutrients. These are either used to make energy, so the body's cells can do their work, or as materials for building and maintaining the body.

The digestive process begins before food enters your mouth. When your stomach is empty, it makes a hormone called ghrelin. This chemical messenger travels through the bloodstream to the hypothalamus in the brain (see page 100), which tells you that you are hungry. When you eat, particularly foods called carbohydrates and proteins, the stomach slows its production of ghrelin so you stop feeling hungry.

The digestive tract is the route that food takes through the body. In an average adult, it is about 9 m (30 ft) long. The tract starts in the mouth and continues through the esophagus (foodpipe), stomach, and intestines. Along the way, the body strips food of its nutrients, which pass into the bloodstream. The journey ends in the rectum, from which smelly waste is expelled from the body as feces (poop).

Several organs help with the digestive process, including the pancreas, which makes digestive enzymes (chemicals that bring about change); and the liver, which makes a liquid called bile to digest fats.

The digestive system breaks food down into glucose (a sugar used by cells to produce energy), amino acids (used by cells for building new materials), and fatty acids and glycerol (used for materials and as energy stores). Food also provides the body with vitamins and minerals, which are materials that it needs to stay healthy. For example, the body uses vitamin C, found in fruits such as oranges and strawberries, for growth and repair. The mineral calcium, found in milk, cheese, and green leafy vegetables, is needed to maintain strong bones and teeth.

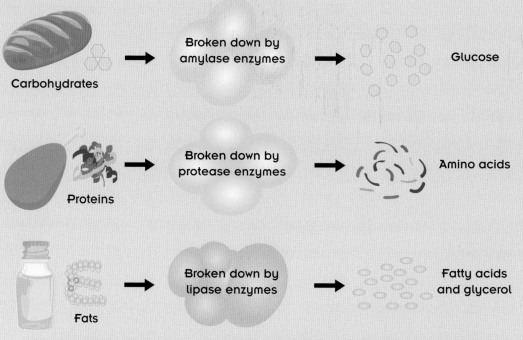

Carbohydrates → Broken down by amylase enzymes → Glucose

Proteins → Broken down by protease enzymes → Amino acids

Fats → Broken down by lipase enzymes → Fatty acids and glycerol

There are three main types of digestive enzymes, each targeting a particular food group. These enzymes break large, complex molecules (groups of joined atoms) into small, simple molecules that can be absorbed and used by cells. Carbohydrates (found in bread) become glucose, proteins (found in chicken) become amino acids, and fats (found in cooking oils) become fatty acids and glycerol.

It takes between 24 and 72 hours for food to travel through the digestive tract, depending on the food and the person, with children usually digesting food faster than adults.

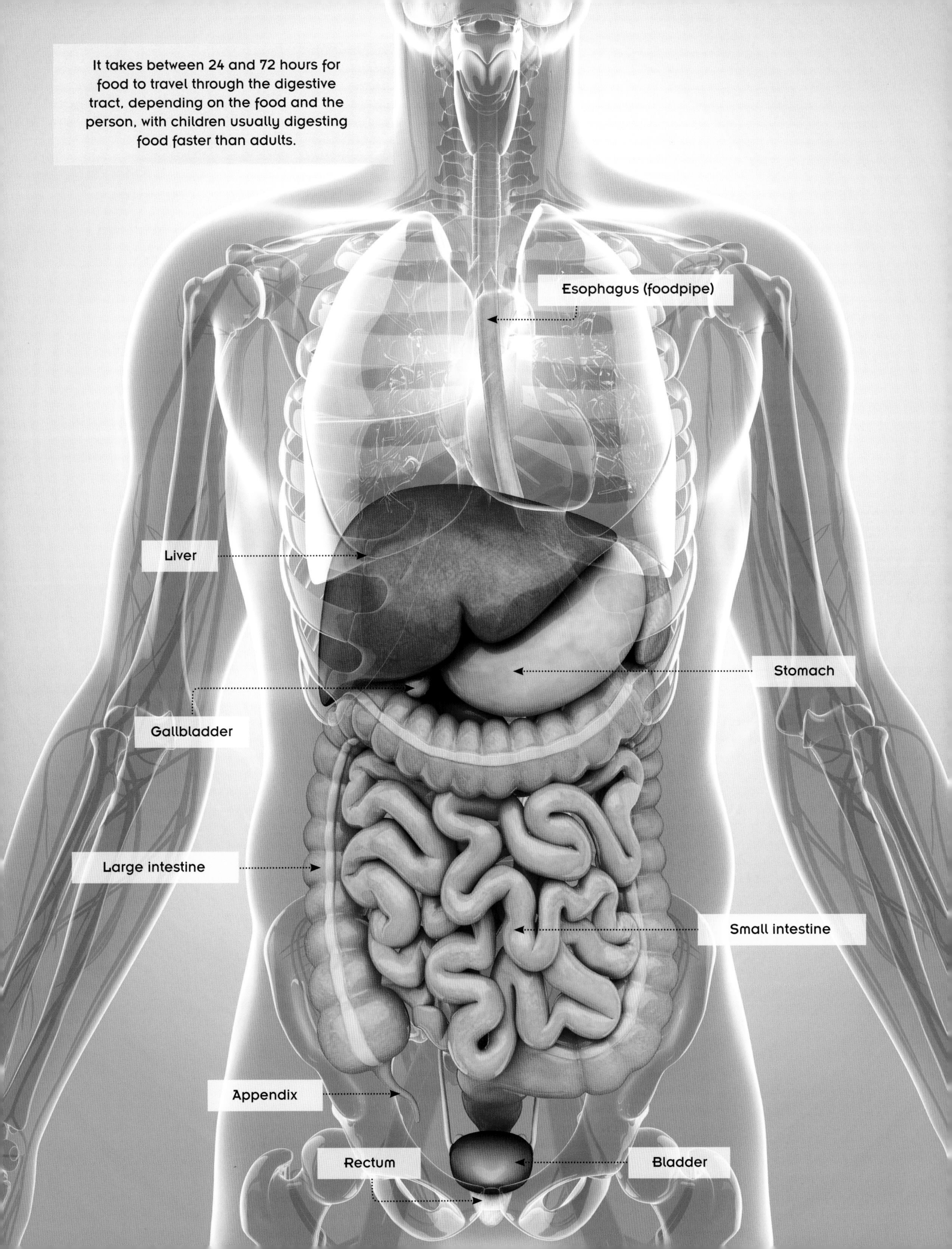

Esophagus (foodpipe)

Liver

Gallbladder

Large intestine

Appendix

Stomach

Small intestine

Rectum

Bladder

MOUTH

Your mouth is the entrance to your digestive system. It begins the digestive process by biting, chewing, moistening, disinfecting, and starting to digest food. In addition, the mouth plays a key role in breathing and speaking.

Anatomy of the mouth

The soft palate is a muscular area that plays a role in swallowing, breathing, and speech.

The tonsils store white blood cells (see page 60) that respond to viruses and bacteria which enter the nose or mouth.

The molars are used for grinding food before it is swallowed.

The eight premolars are used for cutting and chewing food.

The four sharp-tipped canine teeth are used for tearing food.

Composed of muscle running in different directions, the tongue shapes and moves food, as well as helping to make different sounds during speech.

Lips hold and suck food, as well as moving to help speech and non-spoken communication, such as smiling.

There are 32 permanent adult teeth, but children have only 20 baby teeth, which fall out between the ages of 5 and 12 as the adult teeth push on them.

This fleshy projection, called the uvula, helps to close off the nose when swallowing.

Saliva enters the mouth through this duct, as well as through ducts in the upper cheeks and back of the mouth. Saliva moistens food, which makes it easier to swallow. It contains the enzyme amylase, which starts to break down starch, and the enzyme lysozyme, which disinfects food.

The eight incisor teeth are used for biting food.

Biting into really hard foods, such as carrots, can be easier with the broader molars, at the back of the mouth, than the more fragile incisors.

The outer coating of a tooth, called enamel, is the hardest material in the body, containing minerals such as calcium.

Inside a tooth

Enamel and dentine can be broken down by acids, which are made by mouth bacteria that thrive on sugar.

The body's second-hardest tissue is dentine, containing minerals, strong collagen, and water.

The core of the tooth, called pulp, contains blood vessels and nerves, which enable us to feel pain when tooth decay has reached the pulp.

A tooth is surrounded by gum, which is tightly bound to underlying bone.

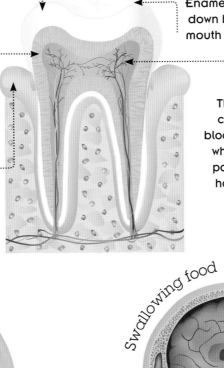

Breathing in

When we breathe in, a flap called the epiglottis is open, letting air flow down the windpipe.

The windpipe leads to the lungs.

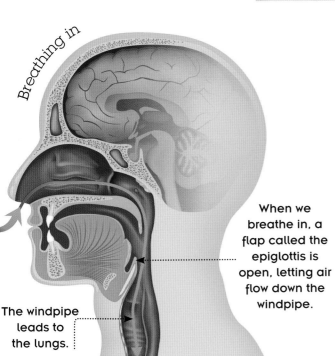

Swallowing food

When we swallow food, the soft palate closes over the entrance to the nose cavity.

The epiglottis closes over the windpipe so food does not enter the lungs.

Food moves down the esophagus toward the stomach.

Teeth

Average adult weight: 1 g (0.035 oz) for an incisor

Main functions: Cutting, tearing, and grinding food

Body system: Digestive

Medical breakthrough: The first modern dental brace, made from wires twisted around the teeth in order to straighten them, was fitted in 1819 by Frenchman Christophe-Francois Delabarre.

An orthodontist specializes in correcting misaligned teeth and jaws, which can help with eating, tooth-cleaning, speech, and appearance.

HEALTHY DIET

Eating a variety of foods is the key to a healthy diet, as each food has its own mix of nutrients: both the macronutrients—carbohydrate, protein, and fat—which your body needs in large quantities; and the micronutrients—vitamins and minerals—that the body needs in small quantities to stay healthy.

Carbohydrates provide your body with glucose, which it converts to energy. Carbohydrates come in different forms, including sugars, fibers, and starches. The healthiest sources of carbohydrates are whole grains (foods made from entire seeds, such as brown rice, wholegrain bread, and wholegrain breakfast cereals), vegetables, fruits, and beans. Less healthy carbohydrates include white bread, cakes, and sweetened drinks, because they contain more sugar and less fiber and starch. However, all foods can have their place in a healthy diet, as long as we try to limit less healthy options and choose the healthy ones when we can.

Going food shopping, choosing recipes, and helping with cooking are great ways to make healthy eating fun.

Food pyramid

A food pyramid shows us how much of each food type we need, with the foods we need most of nearer the bottom.

Healthy fats, such as olive oil, are needed by the body, but foods high in butter, salt, or sugar should be kept as treats for every so often.

Dairy foods, such as milk, yogurt, and cheese, are a source of protein, calcium, and vitamin D.

Fish, meat, nuts, and other sources of protein should cover around an eighth to a quarter of your plate.

Aim for at least three helpings of vegetables a day.

Try to eat plenty of fruit of every color of the rainbow.

Eating a variety of foods is not just healthy but also makes mealtimes more interesting.

You can aim to cover about a third of your plate with whole grains, including bread, pasta, rice, and cereals.

Protein provides the body with materials for producing cells, tissues, and enzymes. Sources of protein include fish, meat (poultry such as chicken is a healthy option), beans, nuts, cheese, and eggs. Fats are also essential to give your body energy and to support cell growth. Fats help your body absorb nutrients and produce hormones. The healthiest sources of fats include vegetable oils, nuts, seeds, and fish. Less healthy fats are animal fats, such as butter and beef or pork fat.

This image captured by an electron microscope shows the lining of the stomach. Mucus-making cells have been tinted brown. Cells that make acid or enzymes are inside pits, which we can see as dark holes.

STOMACH

The stomach is a hollow organ on the upper left side of the abdomen. Its job is to continue the digestion of food, breaking it down into mush with the help of chemicals and its contracting muscles.

Food travels from the throat to the stomach along a tube called the esophagus. The walls of the esophagus are muscly and elastic. The walls squeeze, making a wavelike motion called peristalsis. This pushes balls of chewed food, called boli, down to the stomach.

The stomach is a J-shaped bag. Its walls contain strong muscles that run in different directions from each other, so they can churn food as they contract. Cells in the walls make acid, which kills or damages bacteria in food. Other cells make mucus, which coats the lining of the stomach so it is not damaged by acid. Digestive enzymes are also released, including the protease pepsin, which breaks down proteins. Most nutrients are not absorbed by the stomach, as the job of absorption belongs to the intestines.

After spending 2 to 4 hours in the stomach, food becomes a souplike mush called chyme. At the base of the stomach is a ring of muscle, called a sphincter, through which chyme is squirted in small amounts into the small intestine.

Esophagus

Lower esophageal sphincter

Small intestine

Pyloric sphincter

Stomach

When the lower esophageal sphincter is closed, it prevents acid and food from moving up the esophagus. However, it does relax—and the muscles of the abdomen contract—so you can vomit if you eat something that your body thinks is harmful.

Stomach

Average adult size: 30 cm (12 in) long and 15 cm (6 in) wide when empty

Main functions: Breaking down and disinfecting food; and releasing food to the intestines at a slow and steady rate

Body systems: Digestive and immune

Medical breakthrough: Sores called ulcers can develop on the stomach lining if there is an increase in acid production or decrease in mucus production. In 1982, Australian scientists Robin Warren and Barry Marshall identified an excess of the bacterium *Helicobacter pylori,* usually found in the stomach, as a key cause of the problem.

This illustration shows *Helicobacter pylori* bacteria on the stomach lining. These bacteria have become adapted to living in the acid environment of the stomach.

INTESTINES

The intestines are long, folded tubes that complete the job of digesting food, while absorbing the water and nutrients the body needs. The intestines are in two main parts: the small intestine, so-called because it is narrow, around 2.5 cm (1 in) wide; and the large intestine, around 7.5 cm (3 in) wide.

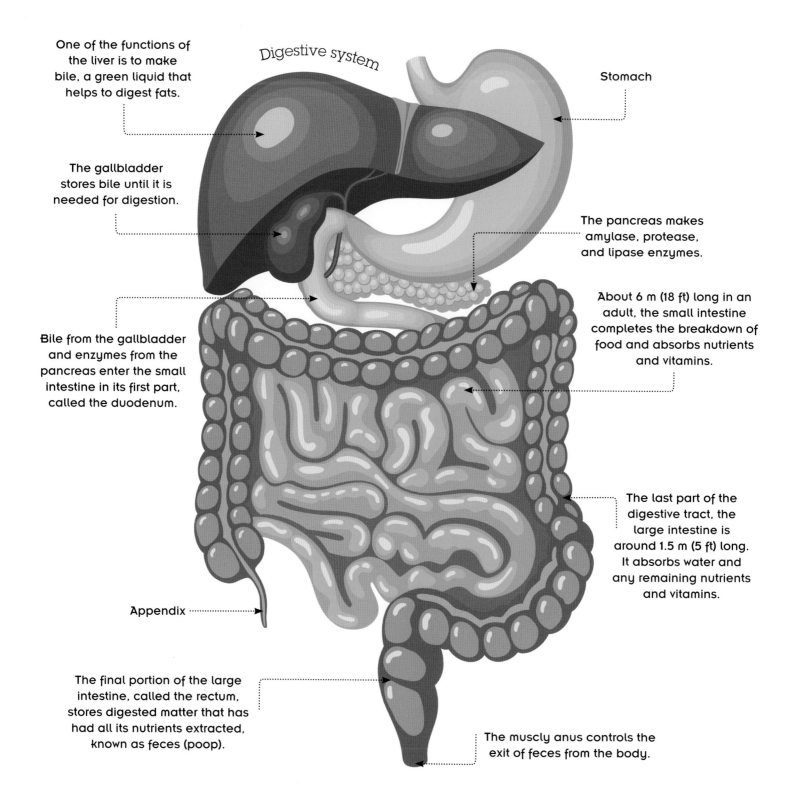

Digestive system

One of the functions of the liver is to make bile, a green liquid that helps to digest fats.

The gallbladder stores bile until it is needed for digestion.

Bile from the gallbladder and enzymes from the pancreas enter the small intestine in its first part, called the duodenum.

Appendix

The final portion of the large intestine, called the rectum, stores digested matter that has had all its nutrients extracted, known as feces (poop).

Stomach

The pancreas makes amylase, protease, and lipase enzymes.

About 6 m (18 ft) long in an adult, the small intestine completes the breakdown of food and absorbs nutrients and vitamins.

The last part of the digestive tract, the large intestine is around 1.5 m (5 ft) long. It absorbs water and any remaining nutrients and vitamins.

The muscly anus controls the exit of feces from the body.

Small intestine

The wall has many folds, which help to increase its surface for absorbing nutrients.

Finger-shaped villi, 0.5–1.6 mm (0.02–0.06 in) long, increase the surface of the small intestine even more.

Microvilli, just 0.001 mm (0.00004 in) long, increase the enterocyte's surface.

The walls of the small intestine are lined with muscles, which push partly digested material along through peristalsis.

Lymphatic vessels (see page 59) absorb digested fats.

An enterocyte is a cell with the job of absorbing nutrients, water, and vitamins.

Nutrients pass into tiny veins, which join the portal vein to travel to the liver (see page 81).

Large intestine

Transverse colon

By the time digested food enters the large intestine, in the region called the cecum, it is almost entirely waste, but some water, minerals, and vitamins remain to be absorbed.

Descending colon

Feces contain water, food that could not be digested, waste from body processes, and billions of bacteria that were living in the intestines. It is these bacteria that make it essential to wash your hands thoroughly after going to the toilet.

Appendix

The ascending colon pushes waste upward through peristalsis, while mucus-making cells ease its journey.

When waste enters the sigmoid colon, it is usually quite dry and compacted.

Feces are expelled from the anus along with gas created by helpful intestine bacteria as they fermented (broke down) waste.

Rectum

Average adult length: 12 cm (4.7 in) long

Main functions: Storing feces until it is appropriate to relax the anus, and sending signals to the brain when full

Body systems: Digestive

Medical breakthrough: The chemical skatole was discovered in 1877 by German doctor Ludwig Brieger. Largely responsible for the strong smell of feces, skatole is produced by helpful bacteria that live in the large intestine as they break down amino acids.

Under a microscope, we can see many mucus-making cells (tinted turquoise) in the lining of the rectum, which helps the passage of feces.

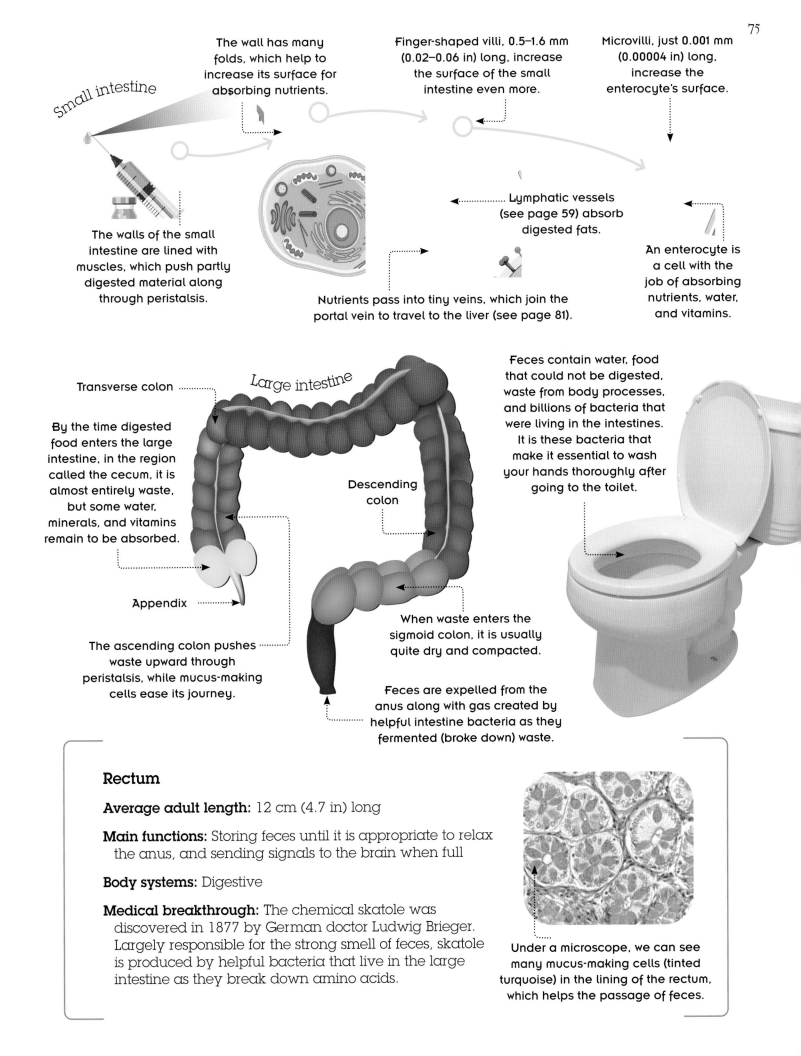

APPENDIX

The appendix is sometimes called a vestigial organ, which means it was useful in our long-ago ancestors but has no use today. However, doctors now believe that it does have a job to do: housing bacteria that help with digestion.

The appendix is a narrow pouch that connects with the cecum of the large intestine, on the lower right side of the abdomen. Scientists think that long ago, when our ancestors ate a more plant-based diet, the appendix was part of a structure that helped to digest tough vegetation.

It was not until 2007 that doctors realized the appendix acts as a safe haven for useful bacteria when illness has flushed bacteria from the rest of the intestines. The surviving bacteria then repopulate the intestines. Trillions of bacteria and other tiny living things, such as fungi, live in the intestines. They have a symbiotic relationship with the body, which means it is a relationship with benefits for both parties. The bacteria digest materials that the body finds hard to break down, such as starches and fiber. This generates energy for themselves and releases nutrients that are absorbed into the blood. The appendix also houses white blood cells that fight harmful invaders that make it as far as the large intestine.

Sometimes, the appendix becomes inflamed, causing a painful condition known as appendicitis. Usually, surgeons carry out an operation to remove the appendix. People who have had their appendix removed do not suffer from ill effects.

Bacteroides species are some of the intestines' most common helpful bacteria, helping to break down sugars.

Lactobacillus species make chemicals that damage harmful bacteria.

The intestines contain over a hundred different types of helpful bacteria, but a few bacteria found in food can be harmful.

Some types of *Escherichia coli* can cause vomiting.

Salmonella bacteria cause serious food poisoning.

Appendix

Average adult length: 9 cm (3.5 in) long

Main functions: Offering a safe haven for useful bacteria, and housing white blood cells

Body systems: Digestive and immune

Medical breakthrough: In 1735, French surgeon Claudius Amyand performed the first successful operation to remove an appendix. The patient was an 11-year old boy named Hanvil Anderson, who had punctured his appendix by swallowing a pin.

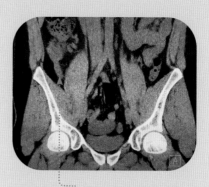

This computed tomography (CT) scan of the abdomen shows an inflamed appendix.

Millions of years ago, our ancient ancestors ate a mostly
plant-based diet, which they digested with the help
of their appendix. Today, leafy greens remain
a key part of a healthy diet.

SURGERY

Surgery, also called an operation, is when a team of highly trained doctors and nurses use tools to work on a patient's body. They may treat an injury, remove unhealthy tissue, fix the functioning of an organ—or even replace an organ, which is called a transplant.

Doctors trained in the use of anesthetics give the patient a local anesthetic, which numbs the body part that will be operated on, or a general anesthetic, which enables the patient to sleep through the operation painlessly. These doctors stay throughout the operation to watch over their patient and make sure they feel calm and happy if they have had a local anesthetic.

Surgeons may use a knife called a scalpel to cut into the body. Clamps prevent blood vessels from bleeding. Forceps (pictured) are used for holding. When the surgeons' work is done, they sew, staple, or glue the cut tissue together. Your body heals the wound over the next few weeks and months.

Before surgery, doctors and nurses wash their hands and put on caps, masks, and gloves so that microorganisms cannot infect the patient.

Machines keep track of the patient's heartbeat, breathing, and blood pressure.

The first operations took place at least 5,000 years ago. Ancient Egyptian doctors carried out surgery to fix broken bones and sew together wounds. In the past, operations were both risky and painful. It was not until the 19th century that doctors realized that tiny living things—called microorganisms, such as bacteria—could infect a wound, causing illness. In 1865, the Scottish surgeon Joseph Lister was the first to place an antiseptic (slowing the spread of microorganisms) called carbolic acid on a patient's wound. Ancient peoples used herbs, roots, seeds, and alcohol to numb pain during an operation, calm the patient, or send them to sleep. From the 19th century, safe and effective anesthetics were developed, including the gas nitrous oxide, which is breathed in, and propofol, which is injected.

In this 15th-century Turkish illustration, a surgeon and his assistant are removing a cyst (fluid-filled sac) from under a patient's tongue.

Surgical nurses help surgeons by handing them the right instruments, which have been sterilized so all microorganisms have been killed.

Worldwide, one of the most commonly performed surgeries is a cesarean section, in which a baby is taken safely out of its mother's womb by making a cut in her abdomen. Other common surgeries include the removal of an appendix, called an appendectomy; cataract surgery, which removes a cloudy lens from the eye; and biopsies, which take a small amount of tissue to check for disease. The first successful organ transplant, of a kidney, was performed in 1954.

Bioprinter

Today, scientists are working on bioprinting, which will one day let working organs be printed using human cells.

This computed tomography (CT) scan shows the liver (dark pink, at the upper left), above the kidneys (yellow), small intestine (pink), and large intestine (blue).

LIVER

One of the liver's many jobs is to filter the nutrient-rich blood arriving direct from the intestines. This busy organ separates harmful toxins from nutrients. It stores some nutrients and sends the rest to the heart for pumping round the body.

Nutrient-rich blood from the intestines travels to the liver along the portal vein. The liver contains millions of liver cells, called hepatocytes. It is the job of these cells to sort through the blood for materials the body does not want, materials it needs right now, and materials it might need in the future.

Nutrients the body needs immediately are sent along the hepatic vein to the heart. The liver stores some nutrients in case food is in short supply in the future. Hepatocytes package and store some glucose as a substance called glycogen. The hepatocytes also store some vitamins and minerals such as iron and copper, which may be useful to the immune system.

Toxins that arrive in the liver include waste from medications. When the hepatocytes come across toxins, they convert them into more harmless waste products and send them to the kidneys. One waste product is called urea, which is a result of the process of breaking down proteins.

Hepatic vein

Liver

Gallbladder

Portal vein

The liver contains thousands of hexagonal lobules, each of which contains thousands of hepatocytes.

The liver is divided into unequally sized left and right parts, called lobes, joined by a ligament.

Lobule

At the corner of each lobule is a bile duct that carries bile to the gallbladder, a tiny artery bringing blood from the heart, and a tiny vein bringing blood from the intestines.

A central vein carries nutrient-rich blood to the heart.

Liver

Average adult weight: 1.4 kg (3.1 lb)

Main functions: Filtering blood from the intestines; neutralizing toxins and sending them to the kidneys; storing glycogen, minerals, and vitamins; making glucose from glycogen stores when needed; making bile to digest fats in the small intestine; making hormones that aid cell growth and platelet production; making proteins that help the blood to clot

Body systems: Digestive, immune, cardiovascular, and endocrine

Medical breakthrough: The liver can be scarred by constant attack from toxins such as alcohol. In 2021, scientists tried out a new treatment, which involves swallowing tiny carbon beads that can soak up toxins.

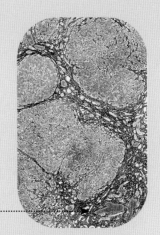

Scarring of the liver is called cirrhosis. Under a microscope, you can see scar tissue (dark areas) growing between the liver lobules (orange areas).

KIDNEYS

The kidneys, bladder, and connecting tubes form the urinary system. This system's role is to filter the blood, removing waste from the body as a liquid called urine—otherwise known as wee or pee.

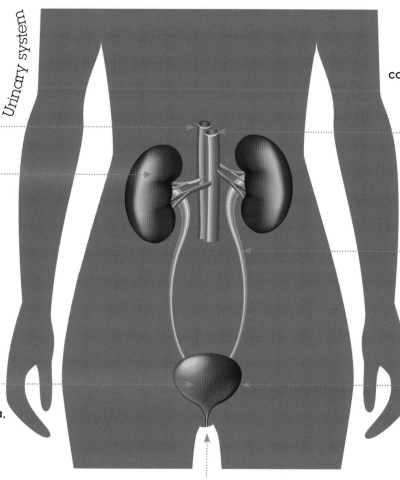

Urinary system

The abdominal aorta carries blood to the kidneys.

The inferior vena cava carries filtered blood away from the kidneys.

The two kidneys filter blood to make sure the amount of water and salts remains constant, while also removing waste products such as urea from the liver and creatine from the muscles.

The filtered-out material, called urine, flows into tubes called ureters.

The inside of the bladder's thick muscly wall has folds called rugae, which stretch out as the bladder fills with urine. In an adult, the bladder can hold up to 600 ml (20 fl oz) of urine before nerves in its walls tell the brain it is time to find a toilet.

Urine is 95 percent water along with urea, salts, creatinine, ammonia, and products of blood breakdown, which give it a pale yellow color.

Urine exits through a tube called the urethra when you relax its muscles.

Kidney

Average adult weight: 150 g (5.3 oz)

Main functions: Filtering and balancing the blood, making hormones that stimulate the production of blood cells and regulate blood pressure, and producing an active form of vitamin D that strengthens bones

Body systems: Urinary, cardiovascular, and endocrine

Medical breakthrough: In 1842, while studying a kidney under a microscope, the English surgeon William Bowman was the first to identify the nephron's cuplike sac, which is named after him.

Three body structures are named after Bowman: Bowman's capsule; Bowman's glands, in the nose; and Bowman's membrane, in the cornea of the eye.

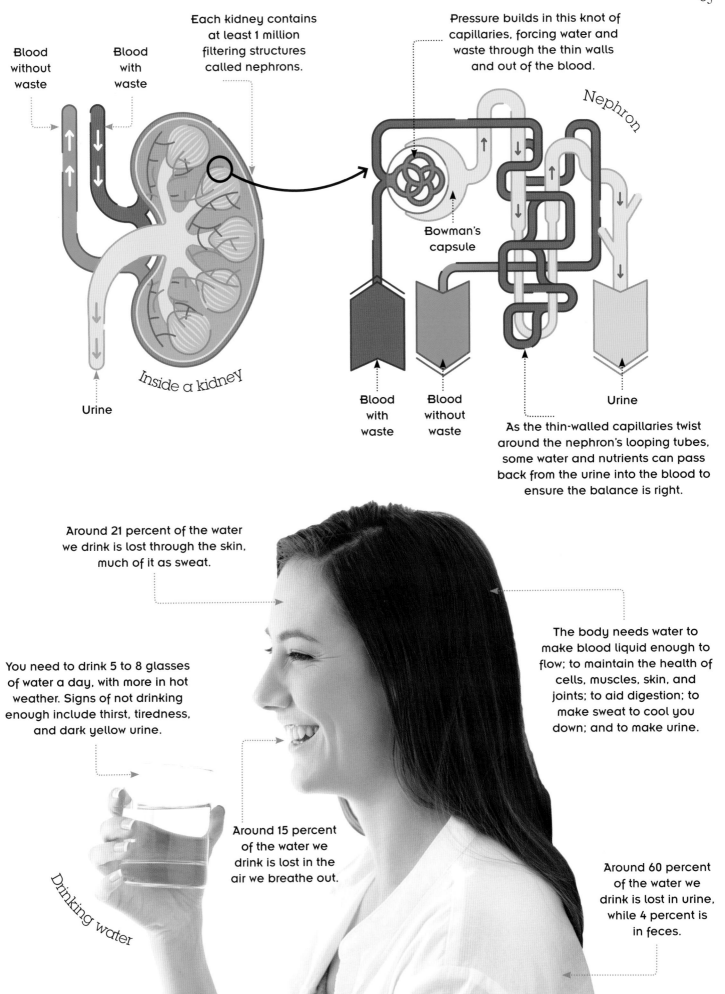

Blood without waste

Blood with waste

Each kidney contains at least 1 million filtering structures called nephrons.

Pressure builds in this knot of capillaries, forcing water and waste through the thin walls and out of the blood.

Nephron

Bowman's capsule

Inside a kidney

Urine

Blood with waste

Blood without waste

Urine

As the thin-walled capillaries twist around the nephron's looping tubes, some water and nutrients can pass back from the urine into the blood to ensure the balance is right.

Around 21 percent of the water we drink is lost through the skin, much of it as sweat.

You need to drink 5 to 8 glasses of water a day, with more in hot weather. Signs of not drinking enough include thirst, tiredness, and dark yellow urine.

The body needs water to make blood liquid enough to flow; to maintain the health of cells, muscles, skin, and joints; to aid digestion; to make sweat to cool you down; and to make urine.

Drinking water

Around 15 percent of the water we drink is lost in the air we breathe out.

Around 60 percent of the water we drink is lost in urine, while 4 percent is in feces.

VACCINATIONS

Vaccinations prevent you from becoming seriously ill with particular diseases. Vaccines work by giving the body weakened or inactive parts of a pathogen (something that causes disease). This helps the immune system develop protection against the disease without making you ill.

The British doctor Edward Jenner pioneered the use of vaccines. In 1796, he gave a smallpox vaccine to an eight-year-old boy called James Phipps. At the time, smallpox—which had symptoms including a blistery rash—caused around 10 percent of all deaths and left survivors with scars. Jenner's vaccine was made from a related but milder virus, cowpox. By injecting the boy with cowpox, his immune system (see page 58) made antibodies that could recognize and attack smallpox. Following a worldwide vaccination program, smallpox was eradicated (wiped out), in 1977. Today, in much of the world, we can be vaccinated against deadly diseases including polio, tetanus, whooping cough, diphtheria, hepatitis B, and meningitis.

Jenner's vaccine, made from cowpox blisters, was scratched into Phipps's skin.

After being vaccinated, James Phipps was exposed to smallpox but did not become ill.

When a large percentage of a population has been vaccinated against a disease, the population has herd immunity. This means that, thanks to all the people who got the vaccine, even if someone has not been vaccinated they are unlikely to catch the disease because they have less chance of meeting an infected person. This helps people with serious health problems, such as cancer, who cannot get a vaccine because even a weakened version of the pathogen could harm them.

In 2020, there was a race against time to produce a vaccine against the virus that causes COVID-19, which had led to a pandemic (when a disease has spread across the world). At record-breaking speed, several successful vaccines had been developed by the end of the year. Rather than using a weakened version of the pathogen itself, some of the vaccines worked by a new method, using mRNA (messenger ribonucleic acid), which gives cells instructions to make proteins. The mRNA in a vaccine teaches the body's cells to make a protein that triggers an immune response to the pathogen.

COVID-19 mRNA vaccine

Specialized mRNA enters the bloodstream.

Cells are instructed to make a spike protein that is found on the surface of the virus.

Immune system cells produce antibodies that can latch onto the spike protein.

If the person is then infected with the virus, their antibodies latch onto the virus, neutralizing it so they get a milder form of the disease or do not become ill at all.

Today, most vaccines are delivered by an intramuscular injection (which uses a needle to put a liquid vaccine into a muscle) or a subcutaneous injection (into the fatty tissue under the skin). Some vaccines can be given as drops on the tongue or a spray up the nose.

Some people have side-effects from a vaccination, such as mild soreness at the site of the injection.

It takes around 7 to 21 days after a vaccination for our immune system to arm itself against the pathogen, giving us immunity.

Chapter 5

THE BRAIN

Your brain is responsible for your conscious thoughts: It enables you to think, talk, move, learn, and remember. But without you being conscious of its work, your brain is also constantly receiving messages from the other organs and the senses, then sending out commands to keep your body safe and well. The brain, spinal cord, and nerves form the body's nervous system.

The brain is your body's most protected organ. Beneath the skin of your scalp, the brain is protected by the bones of the skull. Beneath the skull are three layers of strong, fibrous tissue called the meninges. Between the second and third layers is a cavity through which flows a watery liquid called cerebrospinal fluid. This liquid acts like a cushion, to protect the brain from injury, as well as keeping it supplied with nutrients.

The brain has three main parts: cerebrum, cerebellum, and brainstem. The outer, and largest, part of the brain is the cerebrum (meaning "brain" in Latin). The cerebrum's deeply wrinkled surface, called the cerebral cortex, is where most of our conscious thinking takes place. It is divided into left and right halves, known as hemispheres, which are connected to each other by a bundle of nerves called the corpus callosum. Beneath the cerebrum's surface are structures including the hypothalamus, which controls functions such as sleep; and the hippocampus, which plays a role in memory and emotion.

The cerebellum (meaning "little brain" in Latin) is at the base of your brain. Without your being aware of it, the cerebellum helps with co-ordinating all your movements, including the movements of your eyes. The brainstem is a stalk-shaped structure at the core of your brain. It is positioned where your brain meets the spinal cord, the nerve highway along which signals travel from and to the brain. The brainstem controls your vital functions, such as heartbeat and breathing.

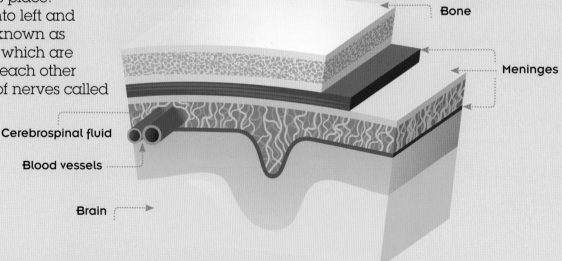

Bone

Meninges

Cerebrospinal fluid

Blood vessels

Brain

From top to bottom, the three layers of the meninges are called the dura mater, arachnoid mater, and pia mater.

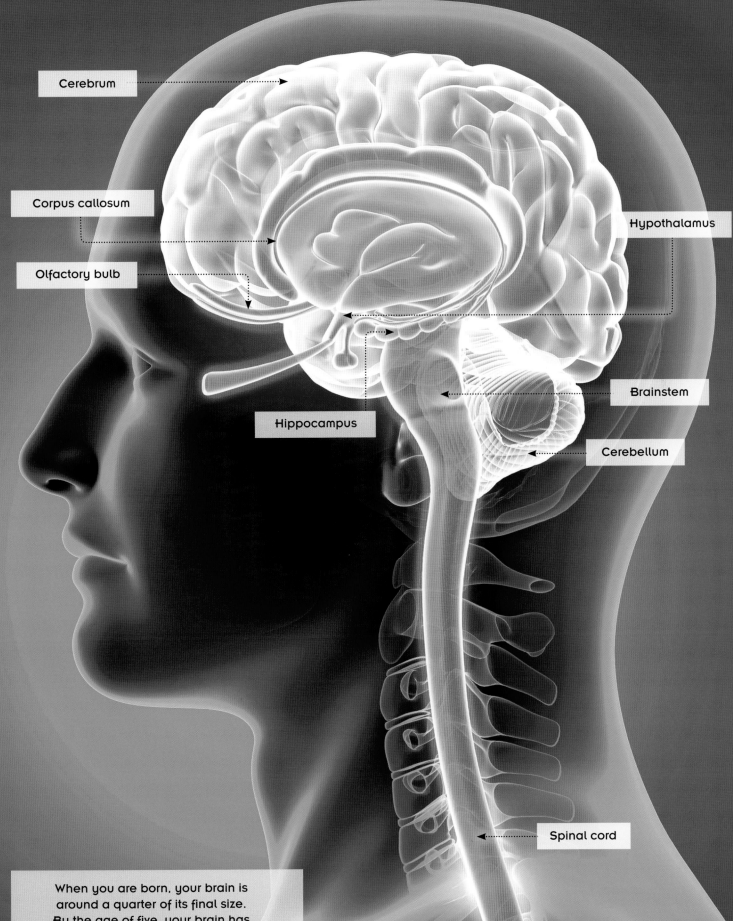

Cerebrum

Corpus callosum

Olfactory bulb

Hypothalamus

Hippocampus

Brainstem

Cerebellum

Spinal cord

When you are born, your brain is around a quarter of its final size. By the age of five, your brain has almost stopped growing larger.

BRAIN CELLS

There are two main types of brain cells: neurons (also called nerve cells) and glial cells. You have around 100 billion neurons, which pass on electrical signals to each other, creating thoughts and memories. Your glial cells provide your neurons with support and nutrients. The different types of glial cells include astrocytes, oligodendrocytes, and microglia.

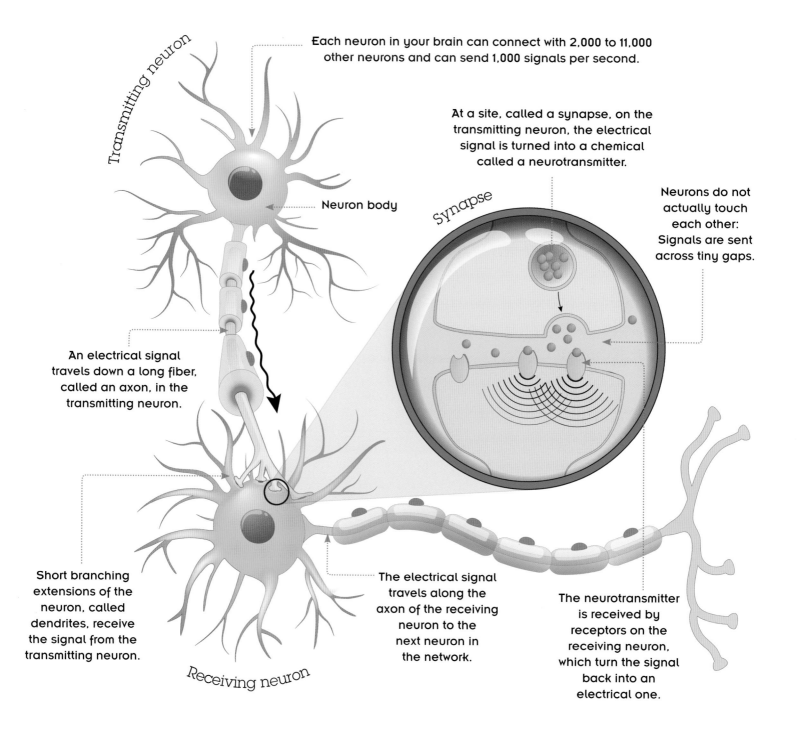

Transmitting neuron

Each neuron in your brain can connect with 2,000 to 11,000 other neurons and can send 1,000 signals per second.

At a site, called a synapse, on the transmitting neuron, the electrical signal is turned into a chemical called a neurotransmitter.

Neuron body

Synapse

Neurons do not actually touch each other: Signals are sent across tiny gaps.

An electrical signal travels down a long fiber, called an axon, in the transmitting neuron.

Short branching extensions of the neuron, called dendrites, receive the signal from the transmitting neuron.

Receiving neuron

The electrical signal travels along the axon of the receiving neuron to the next neuron in the network.

The neurotransmitter is received by receptors on the receiving neuron, which turn the signal back into an electrical one.

CEREBRUM

The cerebrum is what makes you into a unique one-and-only you: It is where you think, make decisions, and store memories. The cerebrum accounts for nearly 90 percent of the weight of your brain.

The surface layer of the cerebrum, around 3 mm (0.12 in) thick, is called the cerebral cortex. This is where most of your higher-level processes take place (see page 92). The cerebral cortex is made of what is often called gray matter because of its color. Gray matter is largely composed of the bodies of neurons and tiny blood vessels.

The cerebral cortex is deeply folded. Millions of years ago, our distant ancestors had much smoother cerebral cortexes. As we grew more intelligent, our cerebral cortexes folded to fit within our skulls. Some of the folds run deep into the brain, forming fissures. The largest fissure, called the medial longitudinal fissure, divides the cerebrum into two hemispheres (see page 96).

Below its surface, the cerebrum is made of what is often called white matter: glial cells and the axons of neurons, which carry signals from one part of the brain to another. In this region are several structures—including the hippocampus (see page 95), amygdala (see page 95), and hypothalamus (see page 100)—that are involved with complex activities such as memory, emotion, and producing hormones.

These structures receive information from the rest of the nervous system, make adjustments, then pass it on to other areas of the brain.

Gyrus (plural "gyri")

The wrinkled texture of the cerebral cortex is formed by many gyri (ridges) and sulci (valleys).

Sulcus (plural "sulci")   Fissure

Cerebrum

Average adult weight: 1.1 kg (2.4 lb)

Main functions: Enabling speech, reasoning, problem-solving, imagination, and learning; storing memories; processing information from the senses; initiating and co-ordinating movement; generating emotions; and regulating hormones and temperature

Body systems: Nervous and endocrine

Medical breakthrough: In the 5th century BC, the ancient Greek thinker and scientist Alcmaeon of Croton was the first to write that the brain is the organ of the mind. Earlier, and many later, scientists thought that the heart was the home of intelligence.

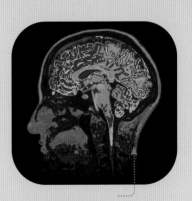

This magnetic resonance imaging (MRI) scan reveals the gyri of the cerebral cortex.

LOBES

Each hemisphere of the cerebral cortex is divided into four lobes, or regions, by fissures. Although activities, from talking to dancing, involve several different parts of the brain, scientists have discovered that the four lobes are related to specific functions. They have also discovered that portions of each lobe are focused on particular activities.

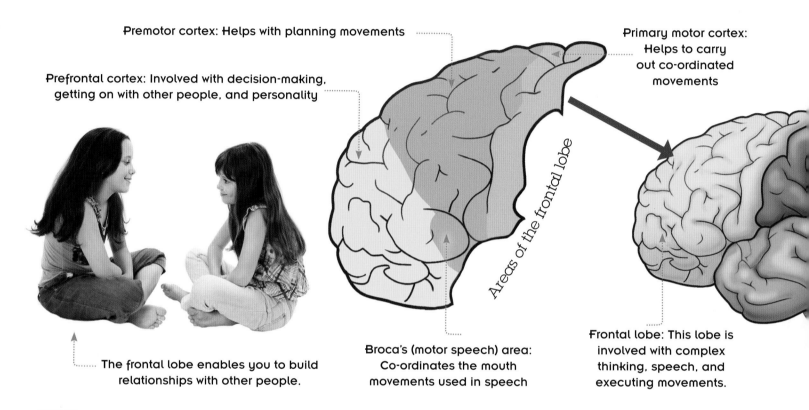

Premotor cortex: Helps with planning movements

Prefrontal cortex: Involved with decision-making, getting on with other people, and personality

Primary motor cortex: Helps to carry out co-ordinated movements

Areas of the frontal lobe

The frontal lobe enables you to build relationships with other people.

Broca's (motor speech) area: Co-ordinates the mouth movements used in speech

Frontal lobe: This lobe is involved with complex thinking, speech, and executing movements.

Broca's area

Length: 2.5 cm (1 in) wide

Main functions: Co-ordinating the muscles of the throat, cheeks, lips, jaws, and tongue to form speech sounds; regulating the breathing while speaking; helping to find words and build sentences; communicating with other areas of the brain involved with speaking and understanding speech; and co-ordinating hand movements made while speaking

Body system: Nervous

Medical breakthrough: In 1861, surgeon Paul Broca identified the motor speech area of the brain through examining, after their death, the brains of patients who had had difficulties with speaking. Broca found damage to the region that has since been known as Broca's area. Righthanded people (see page 96) have their Broca's area only in the left side of their brain, while some lefthanded people have it on their right side.

When a baby learns to form their first words, their Broca's area is working hard.

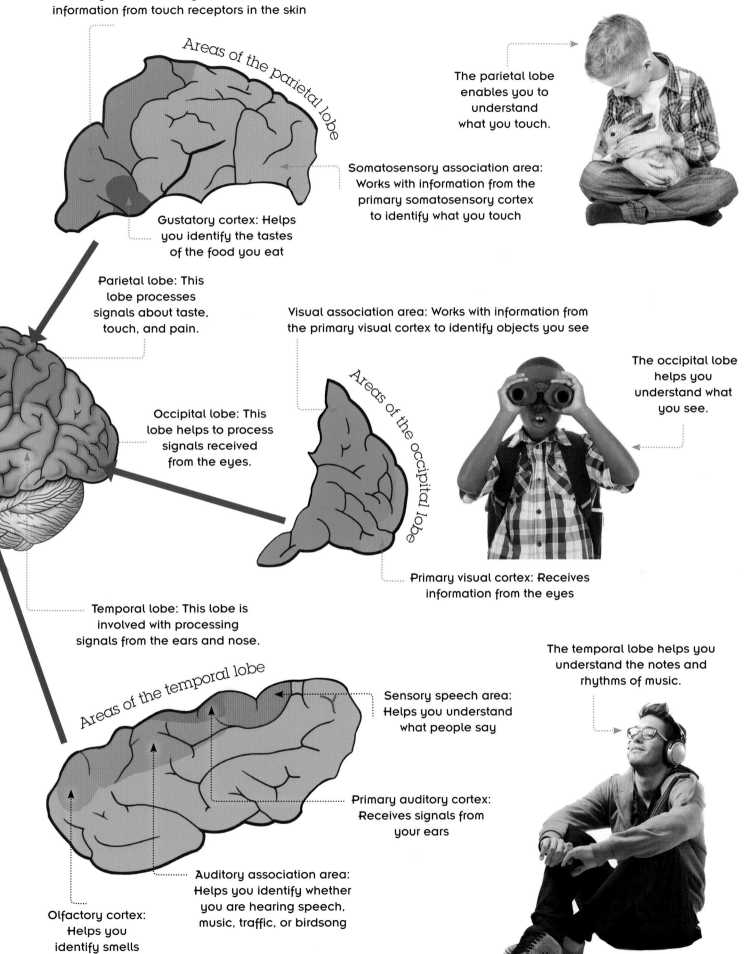

Primary somatosensory cortex: Receives information from touch receptors in the skin

Areas of the parietal lobe

The parietal lobe enables you to understand what you touch.

Somatosensory association area: Works with information from the primary somatosensory cortex to identify what you touch

Gustatory cortex: Helps you identify the tastes of the food you eat

Parietal lobe: This lobe processes signals about taste, touch, and pain.

Visual association area: Works with information from the primary visual cortex to identify objects you see

Occipital lobe: This lobe helps to process signals received from the eyes.

Areas of the occipital lobe

The occipital lobe helps you understand what you see.

Primary visual cortex: Receives information from the eyes

Temporal lobe: This lobe is involved with processing signals from the ears and nose.

The temporal lobe helps you understand the notes and rhythms of music.

Areas of the temporal lobe

Sensory speech area: Helps you understand what people say

Primary auditory cortex: Receives signals from your ears

Auditory association area: Helps you identify whether you are hearing speech, music, traffic, or birdsong

Olfactory cortex: Helps you identify smells

MEMORY

Memory is your brain's ability to store information—and then find it again. Without memory, you would not be able to speak, have friendships, or know who you are. A new memory is created by neurons connecting with each other in a new formation.

"Knowing how"

There are two main types of memories: "knowing what" and "knowing how." "Knowing what" memories are facts you learn, such as "Madrid is the capital of Spain," or memories of events, such as a birthday party you enjoyed. We are less conscious of our "knowing how" memories, but they are at least as important. They include memories for skills and habits, such as how to ride a bicycle or that you eat lunch after morning lessons.

When you learn a new skill, new connections between neurons are formed. The more you practice the skill, the stronger these neuron networks become—and the less effort is needed to perform the skill.

The skill of riding a bike is a "knowing how" memory, also called an unconscious memory.

If an event makes you feel happy, your amygdala adds that emotion to the memory, which makes the hippocampus more likely to store it permanently as connections of neurons.

In a healthy brain, "knowing how" memories are less likely to be lost than "knowing what" memories. You cannot store all your "knowing what" memories for ever, because you would need a much bigger brain. In fact, most information with no long-term use is never stored at all, but kept at hand for up to a minute in what is called the "working memory." For example, as you read a sentence, you hold the beginning of the sentence in your working memory until you read to the end. While the working memory is essential, it is also quite small, which is why you can remember a five-digit security code while you are entering it, but not a ten-digit one.

"Knowing what"

A memory of an event is a "knowing what" memory, also called a conscious memory.

Neuroscientists (scientists who study the brain) think the area that houses working memory is the prefrontal lobe of the cerebral cortex, at the front of your head. The hippocampus is responsible for moving information from the working memory to long-term memory. After processing information, the hippocampus either dismisses it or sends it for storage by neurons in different areas of the brain. Close to the hippocampus is the amygdala, which is responsible for many of your emotions. The amygdala is also responsible for adding emotions to your memories. In fact, the more emotional we feel about an event—joyful, sad, or fearful—the more likely it is to be stored for ever. A part of the brain that processes smells is also nearby, which is why a particular smell may always bring back memories of an event.

The two amygdalas are nut-shaped clusters of neurons deep within the temporal lobes.

There is a hippocampus in each hemisphere of the brain.

Brain structures involved with memory formation

The olfactory bulbs are responsible for linking smells with memories.

CORPUS CALLOSUM

The corpus callosum is a bundle of nerves that links the left and right halves, or hemispheres, of the cerebrum. Each hemisphere has its own lobes and underlying structures. The corpus callosum enables the two halves to work together.

Neuroscientists think the cerebrum is in halves so the hemispheres can specialize in separate processes, but—with the help of the corpus callosum—work together to carry out tasks. The lobes of each hemisphere are not quite mirror images of each other in shape and size (the left hemisphere is larger at the back) and the two hemispheres also have differences in function. The left hemisphere controls the movement of the right side of your body, while receiving information from the right ear and right visual field (the right half of what both eyes see). The right hemisphere controls the left side of the body and gets information from the left ear and left visual field.

When it comes to thinking, the left hemisphere is associated with practical skills, mathematical ability, language, and reasoning. The right side is linked with creativity, emotions, and intuition (understanding with our feelings rather than reasoning).

The corpus callosum is made of the axons of around 250 million neurons. Signals travel along these axons to share information between the two hemispheres, enabling you to walk using both sides of your body and to think using both hemispheres. For example, the left hemisphere is very active while you are doing sums, but the right side is helping you estimate your answers and compare your results.

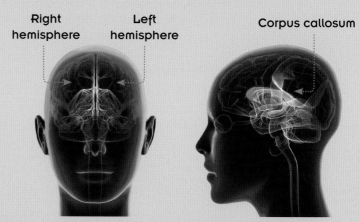

Right hemisphere   Left hemisphere   Corpus callosum

The corpus callosum is a structure found only in humans and other mammals, such as apes and dogs.

Corpus callosum

Average adult size: 10 cm (4 in) long

Main functions: Carrying signals between the left and right hemispheres of the cerebrum

Body system: Nervous

Medical breakthrough: In around 90 percent of people, the left hemisphere is dominant, which makes them righthanded, with their right hand more skilled at performing tasks. Around 10 percent of people are lefthanded. In 2016, researchers studying prehistoric cave paintings noted there have been both left- and righthanded people for thousands of years. They concluded that having right- and lefthanded people in a population is a benefit for everyone as it lets tasks be shared helpfully.

Some of these ancient cave-painters used their right hand to hold a pipe through which they blew paint over their left hand, but a few used their left hand to hold the pipe, suggesting they were lefthanded.

While your left hemisphere is focusing on chores, the right hemisphere is thinking about a TV show you love.

The cerebellum is very active during tightrope walking.

Cerebellum

Located at the back of the brain, the cerebellum has an important role in smoothing and co-ordinating your conscious movements, from walking to throwing a ball. If someone's cerebellum is damaged, they may move clumsily or unsteadily.

The cerebellum does not initiate movement, which is the job of the cerebrum. However, the cerebellum does essential work on co-ordination, accuracy, and timing of movements, enabling you to run, aim a ball at a goal, and even balance on a tightrope. To do its work, the cerebellum receives information direct from the spinal cord about the position of the body and limbs, while also receiving information from the cerebrum and brainstem. The cerebellum processes all these inputs to fine-tune your conscious movements, helping all the different muscles, including the muscles of your eyes, work together.

Even when you are not moving, your cerebellum is working hard to help you balance. It receives information from the inner ear (see page 118) about whether you are upright or leaning, then sends signals to adjust your posture.

Unlike the hemispheres of the cerebrum, the right side of the cerebellum does control the right side of your body, which it does by communicating with the left hemisphere of the cerebrum.

The cerebellum also plays a part in learning to perform movements, as when a child is starting to walk, when you are learning a new sport, or when you adjust all your movements as you grow taller. At first you move clumsily, until the cerebellum adjusts its commands.

Cerebellum

Although the cerebellum is fairly small, it contains more than half of all the brain's neurons.

Cerebellum

Average adult weight: 150 g (5 oz)

Main functions: Fine-tuning conscious movements, balance, and posture; and receiving pain signals from the body then adjusting posture or movements

Body system: Nervous

Medical breakthrough: In 2010, neuroscientists studied how the cerebellum shrinks as we get older, which partly accounts for difficulties with balance and movement in some elderly people.

A healthy diet and regular exercise, such as practicing the Chinese martial art tai chi, can help the cerebellum stay healthy as we age.

HORMONES

Hormones are chemicals that act as messengers in the body. More than fifty different types of hormones regulate all the body's processes, from sleeping and eating to growing and reproducing. The brain controls the release of hormones.

Hormones are made in special hormone-producing organs called glands, as well as in other organs that make hormones alongside other work. All these organs are part of the endocrine system, the body's hormone system. The endocrine system is controlled by a brain structure called the hypothalamus, deep inside the cerebrum. The hypothalamus gathers information received by the brain, such as about temperature, light, and feelings. It then communicates with the nearby pituitary gland by sending it hormones. When the pituitary gland receives these signals, it releases hormones that control many of the other endocrine glands. When glands receive a signal to produce a particular hormone, they release it into the bloodstream. Only cells that are receptive to a particular hormone will respond to it, by starting to behave differently.

Endocrine system

Pineal gland: When signals from the eyes tell the brain it is dark, the pineal gland produces melatonin, which makes you feel sleepy.

Hypothalamus: The hypothalamus controls the endocrine system by producing hormones it sends to the pituitary gland.

Pituitary gland: The pituitary gland stores and releases hormones made by the hypothalamus, makes hormones that signal to the other endocrine organs, and produces growth hormones that develop the bones and muscles.

Thyroid gland: This gland makes hormones that control appetite and the speed of digestion as well as heart rate.

Thymus: This organ produces the hormone thymosin, which makes white blood cells develop.

Adrenal glands: These glands produce adrenaline, which triggers the flight or fight response (see opposite).

Pancreas: The pancreas makes insulin, which tells the cells of muscles, the liver, and fat to store glucose sugar, controlling the level of sugar in the blood.

Ovaries: In a woman, the ovaries produce hormones that control the reproductive cycle.

Cuddle hormone

The hypothalamus makes the hormone oxytocin, which is stored in the pituitary gland and released in large quantities when a mother cuddles her baby, making her feel happy. Your pituitary gland also releases oxytocin when you are playing with friends or family.

The flight or fight response can be triggered by situations that are stressful rather than life-threatening, such as starting a new school, sitting a test, or giving a performance, resulting in an unhelpfully pounding heart, shaking limbs, and fluttering stomach (produced by the sudden loss of blood flow).

The endocrine system is in charge of the flight or fight response, which readies us to run or put up a fight when we are under attack. When the hypothalamus receives a signal that you are under threat—for example, from a speeding car—it signals the pituitary gland, which releases a hormone that tells the adrenal glands to release adrenaline. This hormone triggers the speeding up of your heartbeat and breathing; the release of more glucose sugar into the blood; and the direction of blood away from the stomach to the arms and legs. All this gives a sudden burst of energy, enabling you to jump out of the way of the speeding car.

BRAINSTEM

Positioned at the top of the spinal cord, the brainstem is a busy nerve junction, through which pass all signals from and to the brain. The brainstem is truly the core of your brain: It regulates your body's vital processes, your awareness, and your consciousness.

The brainstem is in three main parts: midbrain, pons, and medulla oblongata. The midbrain communicates with the hypothalamus (see page 100) to regulate your sleep and your wakefulness. When you are awake and healthy, the midbrain keeps your alert to your surroundings. In addition, the midbrain controls your response to pain, enabling you to bear low levels of it.

The pons portion of the brainstem, which is directly linked to the face through nerve pathways, is involved with controlling your facial expressions. It also initiates the periods of sleep in which you dream, known as rapid eye movement (REM) sleep because your eyes tend to move beneath your closed eyelids.

Neuroscientists believe that REM sleep is essential for storing memories and for processing the events of the day.

It is the medulla oblongata that regulates your breathing and heartbeat, ensuring that both continue constantly, changing speed when you are exercising. This region also regulates other actions that you do not consciously control, such as sneezing (to expel irritants in the nose), coughing (to expel irritants from the airways), vomiting (to expel harmful substances from the stomach), and swallowing. It tells your saliva glands to produce saliva when you see food or start to eat.

Midbrain

Pons

Medulla oblongata

Spinal cord

The brainstem is in charge of the body's processes that are needed for you to stay alive.

Brainstem

Average adult weight: 35 g (1.2 oz)

Main functions: Processing and passing on signals to and from the organs, muscles, and the rest of the brain; controlling your body's unconscious processes; regulating sleep; regulating the brain's response to pain; and keeping you alert when you are awake

Body system: Nervous

Medical breakthrough: In 2021, for the first time, a growth was removed successfully from the brainstem of a 16-year-old girl, using new equipment: a thin, tube-shaped tool that highly trained surgeons can insert into the brain to suck out unwanted tissue.

Signals to the facial muscles travel through the brainstem, from both hemispheres of the cerebrum and from the cerebellum.

The brainstem initiates three to five REM periods of sleep per night, each one lasting up to an hour, whether or not you remember your dreams when you wake.

EMOTIONS

From happiness to embarrassment, we feel emotions nearly every minute of every day. Emotions are born in a region at the heart of your brain called the limbic system, which includes structures such as the amygdala and hippocampus.

An emotion is usually triggered by an experience. As an emotion takes shape in your brain, various changes take place: in your thoughts, your decisions, your facial expression, your body posture and responses (such as tears or laughter), and even the hormones coursing through your bloodstream (see page 100). These changes are helped along by chemicals in the brain, called neurotransmitters, that encourage different patterns of activity. For example, the neurotransmitter serotonin is linked with happiness.

Emotions and the limbic system

Information from the senses is passed to the limbic system.

The cingulate gyrus links our emotions with our actions, helping us to understand which actions (such as working hard) will lead to emotional rewards (such as pride).

By working with our memories, the hippocampus helps us to understand our emotions.

The prefrontal cortex helps us to control and respond to our emotions.

The amygdala processes information from the senses and starts to generate emotions.

Psychologists study the mind and emotions. They believe there are a number of basic, universal emotions, which are felt by most people frequently. Some emotions are pleasant, such as happiness, amusement, desire, pride, awe, relief, and sympathy. Others feel unpleasant, such as sadness, anger, fear, disgust, boredom, and shame. Each of these emotions is linked with particular patterns of activity in the brain, as well as particular thoughts, decisions, and facial expressions. More complex feelings may be mixtures of these basic emotions. For example, love may be a mixture of happiness, pride, and sympathy. Complex emotions, including jealousy and grief, do not always have a recognizable facial expression and so can be harder for other people to identify.

Scientists think that humans have evolved to feel emotions because they help with humankind's survival. Fear protects us from harm, while love encourages us to take care of each other. Often emotions guide us toward behaving kindly, so we can escape the negative feeling of shame. Showing our sadness—particularly through tears—usually makes other people kind to us, just as we try to be kind to them when they need our support.

Sometimes sadness or worry last for a long time, preventing us from enjoying life. Talking about our emotions with family, friends, a teacher, or another trusted adult is the first step to feeling better. Some people may need to talk to a healthcare professional trained to deal with emotional problems.

Amusement is a basic emotion, which we can recognize from its characteristic facial expression (a smile) and other bodily responses, such as laughter.

Chemicals such as serotonin and dopamine are active in the brain, giving a feeling of well-being.

Feeling amusement with friends helps us to bond, which encourages us to work together for everybody's benefit.

Chapter 6

SENSES AND COMMUNICATION

Your body is skilled at interacting with the world around you. Your senses gather information about the world, from the sound of voices to the smell of flowers. Your brain makes sense of this information so you can respond. Your brain also enables you to communicate with other people, through talking, moving, and touching.

Traditionally, humans are said to have five senses: sight, smell, taste, hearing, and touch. Each of these senses has its own sense organs: the eyes, nose, mouth, ears, and skin. Sense organs are groups of cells, called receptors, that respond to a particular type of physical change in the outside world, such as light or sound. Signals from the sense organs are carried along nerves to the brain, where they are processed, identified, and understood.

The brain and spinal cord make up the central nervous system. The spinal cord is a nerve highway that runs through the backbone. A network of nerves spreads out from the brain and spinal cord to carry signals to and from the rest of the body. This network is called the peripheral (meaning "away from the center") nervous system. Twelve pairs of cranial nerves carry signals between the brain and the head and neck, including the organs of sight, smell, taste, and hearing. It is no coincidence that these organs are in the head, with little distance to travel to the brain. Thirty-one pairs of nerves spread out from the spinal cord, branching to reach every part of the body. Signals from

receptors in the skin, about touch and pain, travel along these nerves.

In addition to the traditional senses, which enable us to experience the external world, we have several more senses that enable us to monitor our internal world, inside the body. These detect internal changes using signals from internal organs and tissues. Internal senses include the sense of balance and the sense of body position, also called proprioception. Our feelings of pain, hunger, thirst, and nausea (feeling sick) can also be called senses.

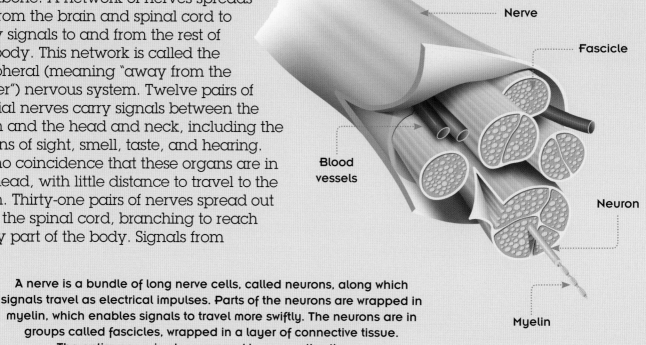

Nerve

Fascicle

Blood vessels

Neuron

Myelin

A nerve is a bundle of long nerve cells, called neurons, along which signals travel as electrical impulses. Parts of the neurons are wrapped in myelin, which enables signals to travel more swiftly. The neurons are in groups called fascicles, wrapped in a layer of connective tissue. The entire nerve is also wrapped in connective tissue.

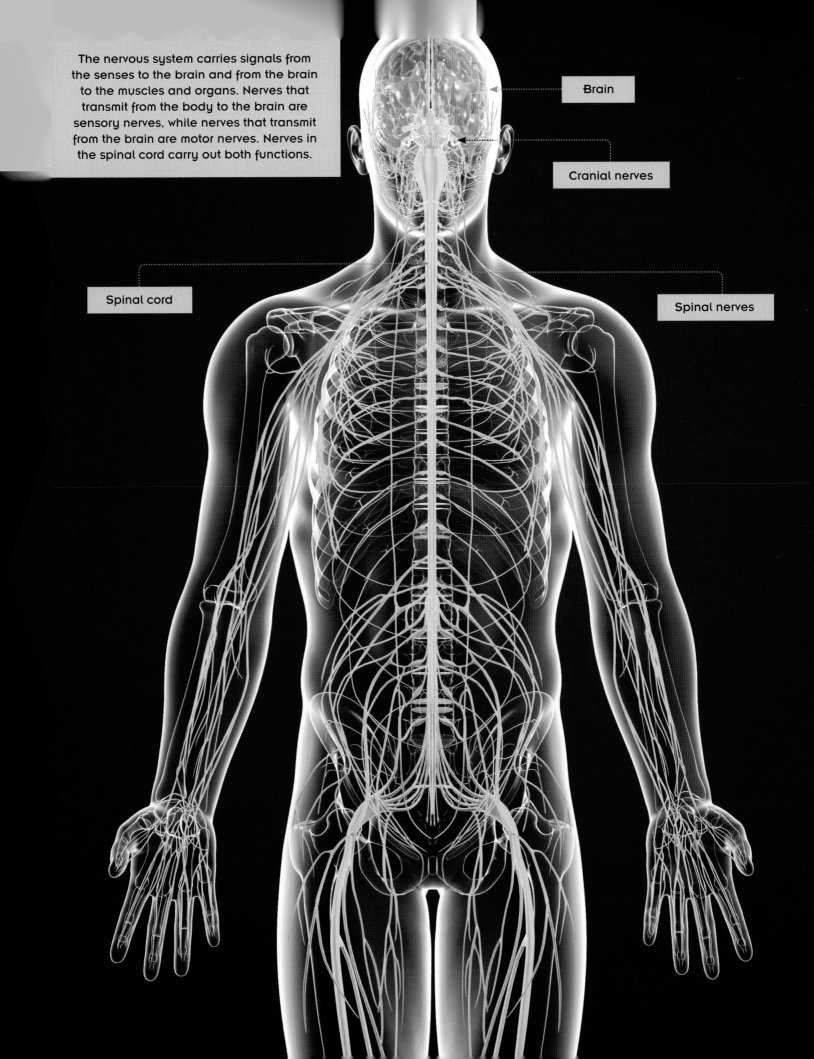

The nervous system carries signals from the senses to the brain and from the brain to the muscles and organs. Nerves that transmit from the body to the brain are sensory nerves, while nerves that transmit from the brain are motor nerves. Nerves in the spinal cord carry out both functions.

Brain

Cranial nerves

Spinal cord

Spinal nerves

SIGHT

You can see because light—from the Sun or a lightbulb—bounces off objects and into your eyes. Your eyes detect patterns of light, using more than 120 million light-sensitive cells, called rods and cones. Signals from these cells travel along the optic nerve to the brain, which makes sense of them to build a picture of the world around you.

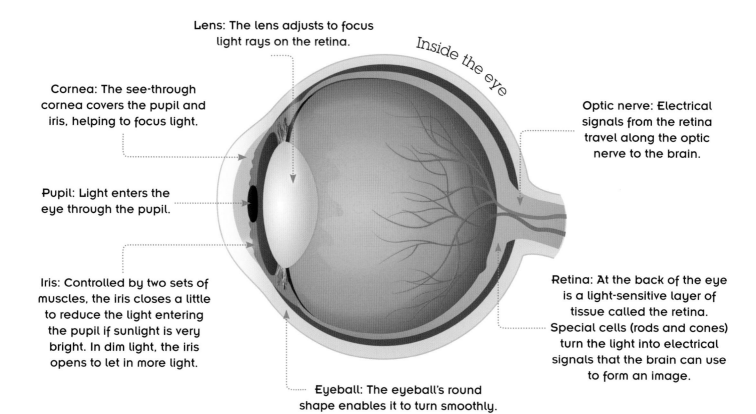

Lens: The lens adjusts to focus light rays on the retina.

Inside the eye

Cornea: The see-through cornea covers the pupil and iris, helping to focus light.

Optic nerve: Electrical signals from the retina travel along the optic nerve to the brain.

Pupil: Light enters the eye through the pupil.

Iris: Controlled by two sets of muscles, the iris closes a little to reduce the light entering the pupil if sunlight is very bright. In dim light, the iris opens to let in more light.

Retina: At the back of the eye is a light-sensitive layer of tissue called the retina. Special cells (rods and cones) turn the light into electrical signals that the brain can use to form an image.

Eyeball: The eyeball's round shape enables it to turn smoothly.

Eye

Average adult size: 2.4 cm (0.9 in) across

Main functions: Collecting light and converting it into electrical signals that are sent to the brain, and helping to communicate meaning and emotion

Body system: Nervous

Medical breakthrough: Through studying a bull's eyeball, the Frenchman René Descartes proved in the 1630s that the image focused on the retina is upside down. The brain processes the information from the retina, making it fit with what it already knows, so we "see" a right-way-up image.

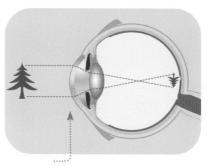

Since the front part of the eye is curved, it bends light, creating an upside-down image on the retina.

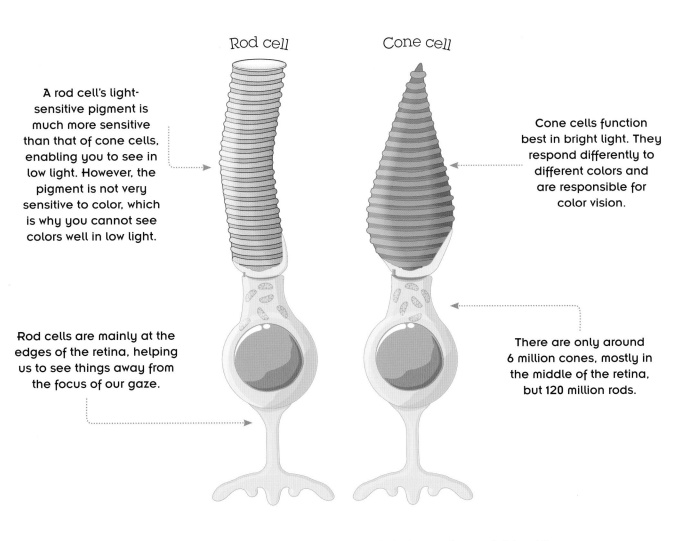

Rod cell

Cone cell

A rod cell's light-sensitive pigment is much more sensitive than that of cone cells, enabling you to see in low light. However, the pigment is not very sensitive to color, which is why you cannot see colors well in low light.

Cone cells function best in bright light. They respond differently to different colors and are responsible for color vision.

Rod cells are mainly at the edges of the retina, helping us to see things away from the focus of our gaze.

There are only around 6 million cones, mostly in the middle of the retina, but 120 million rods.

Sclera: Humans are among the few animals to have a large, visible white area of the eye, known as the sclera. The sclera makes it easier to follow another person's gaze and to communicate with the eyes.

Eyelashes: This fringe of hair protects the eye from dust and sweat.

Lacrimal caruncle: This gland makes sweat and oil to stop the eye from drying out.

Upper eyelid: The eyelid blinks to protect the eye from dust and to spread tears and oil across the eye. At night, it closes to keep the eye moist.

Iris: The iris's color depends on the quantity of the dark pigment melanin, which is also found in skin and hair. Large quantities of melanin create brown irises, while little melanin makes irises blue.

Tear gland: Glands beneath the upper eyelids make most of your tears, composed largely of water and salts, which enter the eye through small openings in the eyelids. Tears constantly keep the eyes moist, remove irritants, and—in larger quantities—are a natural response to pain, sadness, and intense happiness.

Anatomy of the eye

Pupil: The pupil is a hole, which appears black because all light entering is absorbed.

PROPRIOCEPTION

Proprioception is your sense of your body's movement and its position in space. This sense is what enables you to close your eyes then touch the tip of your nose with your finger. At any moment, proprioception is telling your brain where your finger is and where your nose is!

Proprioception is possible because of special nerve cells, called proprioceptors, that are located in your muscles and joints, such as the knee or elbow. Proprioceptors can detect movement in the muscles, position of the joints, and how much effort the muscles and joints are making to lift or pull. When your brain receives these signals, it combines them with information from the eyes and from the sense of balance (see page 118) to create a picture of the whole body's movement, speed, and position.

Sensory nerve: Information about the stretch of the muscle is carried along sensory nerves to the brain.

Detecting muscle stretch

Muscle spindle: Inside your muscles are spindle-shaped (like a stretched lemon) areas of muscle entwined with sensory nerves.

Skeletal muscle

Connective tissue

III

Proprioception enables you to crack an egg with the right amount of strength, so the shell shatters but you do not cover the kitchen with mess!

We are not often conscious of our proprioception at work. Occasionally, you may notice yourself making conscious calculations based on proprioception when carrying out difficult reaches or somersaults. Much of this sense's work is carried out not by the parts of the brain where you do your conscious thinking (the cerebrum) but by the cerebellum (see page 99), where muscle movements are co-ordinated without you being conscious of it.

A gymnast's training fine-tunes their proprioception so they can make leaps, stretches, and catches without falling.

Righting reflex

A cat—nearly always—lands on its feet if it falls.

Proprioception helps you walk without falling over, without having to look at your feet. It also helps you use the correct amount of force in your movements. For example, it enables you to move a cup to your lips without hitting yourself in the face. Proprioception helps with reflexes, which are unconscious movements that keep you safe. For example, the righting reflex makes you adjust your position if your body tips to the side.

The righting reflex can be observed in cats, which have similar proprioception to humans.

Food with a pleasant smell makes you want to eat.
As you bite in, your sense of smell helps you to
enjoy the full experience of food.

SMELL

Your sense of smell helps you to enjoy food and to detect hazards. Smells are detected by receptors inside the nose, which send signals to the brain, where information is processed and sometimes stored as a memory.

A smell is a tiny molecule: a collection of atoms. These molecules are light enough to be carried through the air. The molecules are given off much more easily by some substances, such as food, than by others, such as glass.

Once the smell molecules enter your nostrils, they are dissolved in (floated and spread by) the mucus (snot) that coats the lining of your nose. This helps the molecules to be detected by special cells, called olfactory receptors, near the back of the nose. These receptors send signals along the olfactory nerves to an area at the front of the brain called the olfactory bulb, which determines what kind of molecules are forming the smell. The information then travels to parts of the brain connected with emotion and memory. This is why smells can make you feel disgust, happiness, or even remind you of another time you experienced them. Information is then sent to the part of the brain where we do our thinking, the cerebral cortex. If food smells like it is decaying, the cortex will decide not to put that food into your mouth. If you smell smoke, your cortex decides to raise the alarm.

Your sense of smell also responds to chemicals, called pheromones, that are given off by other people. You never consciously smell pheromones but your brain still responds to them. Brothers and sisters, parents and children, can detect each other's pheromones, helping us feel happy when we are with family.

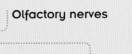

Brain Olfactory bulb

Olfactory nerves

Nose Olfactory receptors

Smell molecules

Different types of olfactory receptors detect different smells, enabling the brain to tell the difference between up to 1 trillion smells.

Nose

Size of olfactory receptor: 0.01 cm (0.004 in) long

Main functions: Detecting smells to keep us safe and to kickstart the digestive process; letting air enter the respiratory tract on its way to the lungs; and making mucus that traps dust, bacteria, and viruses before they can enter the lungs

Body systems: Nervous, digestive, respiratory, and immune

Medical breakthrough: In 1991, scientists Linda Buck and Richard Axel identified how different olfactory receptors change when particular smell molecules attach to them, causing them to send electrical signals to the olfactory bulb.

Under a powerful microscope, you can see the nose lining with an olfactory receptor (tinted red), with hairlike projections that trap mucus and the smell molecules floating in it.

TASTE

When you put food in your mouth, your sense of taste helps you to identify and enjoy it. Around 500,000 taste receptor cells let you know if a food tastes good or bad, which makes you want to eat it—or spit it out!

If you stick out your tongue and look in the mirror, you will see hundreds of small bumps on the tongue's surface, which are called papillae. Most of these bumps contain hundreds of taste buds, each of which contains 50 to 100 taste receptor cells. Taste buds are also found on the roof and sides of the mouth and in the throat.

Taste receptor cells can identify five tastes: sweetness, sourness, saltiness, bitterness, and umami (also called savoriness). Most foods are a unique mixture of all these tastes. Different types of taste receptors respond best to only one or two of the five different tastes. When a taste receptor meets a food molecule that triggers it to react, it sends a signal along a nerve to the brain. The brain processes all the information from the thousands of receptor cells.

Your total understanding of a food's taste is helped along by smell signals from the nose, visual signals from the eyes, and touch signals from the nerves of the face, which tell you about texture, heat, and cold. The senses of taste and smell combine at the back of the throat, where the nose cavity meets the mouth. These two senses are very similar, as they are both responding to chemical molecules. While the taste receptors can identify only five tastes, the olfactory receptors respond to many more different chemicals. This is why, when your nose is clogged by a heavy cold, your food tastes dull and is harder to identify.

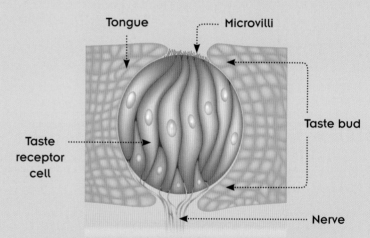

Taste receptor cells have hairlike extensions called microvilli that extend into the mouth to pick up tastes.

Tongue

Average adult weight: 65 g (2.3 oz)

Main functions: Tasting; moving food for chewing; helping with swallowing; and forming sounds during speech

Body systems: Nervous, digestive, and respiratory

Medical breakthrough: In 1907, Japanese chemist Kikunae Ikeda discovered the chemical basis of the taste he named umami. The taste is created by the chemical molecule monosodium glutamate.

Kikunae Ikeda decided that humans enjoy the umami taste because it is linked with protein, a necessary part of our diet. Umami can be tasted strongly in meat soups and stews, mushrooms, cheese, and soy sauce.

While sweet and umami tastes usually make us want to eat more, sour or bitter tastes can provoke disgust. Strongly bitter tastes warn us something could be poisonous.

HEARING

Your ears enable you to hear sounds, from speech to singing and traffic to tambourines. All sounds are made by vibrations, which is shaking so tiny we usually cannot see it. These vibrations travel through the air—or through water—and into our ears.

When you bang a drum, you make the skin of the drum vibrate. This makes the surrounding air molecules vibrate.

When a molecule vibrates, it makes the molecules that are touching it vibrate. The vibration travels through the air in the form of a wave.

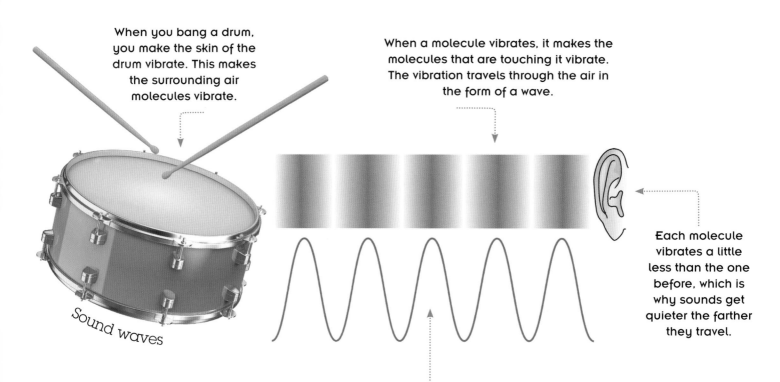

Sound waves

Each molecule vibrates a little less than the one before, which is why sounds get quieter the farther they travel.

A sound wave is a little like a wave on the ocean, with tightly packed molecules making the peaks of the wave and lightly packed molecules making the troughs of the wave.

Ear

Average size of eardrum: 0.9 cm (0.35 in) across

Main functions: Detecting sounds, and helping with balance

Body system: Nervous

Medical breakthrough: The first electric hearing aid was invented by American engineer Miller Reese Hutchison in 1895, for his friend Lyman Gould. The device amplified (or increased) sounds, so they could be heard more easily.

A modern hearing aid amplifies sound and directs it into the ear, while also adjusting to the user's type of hearing loss and the level of background noise.

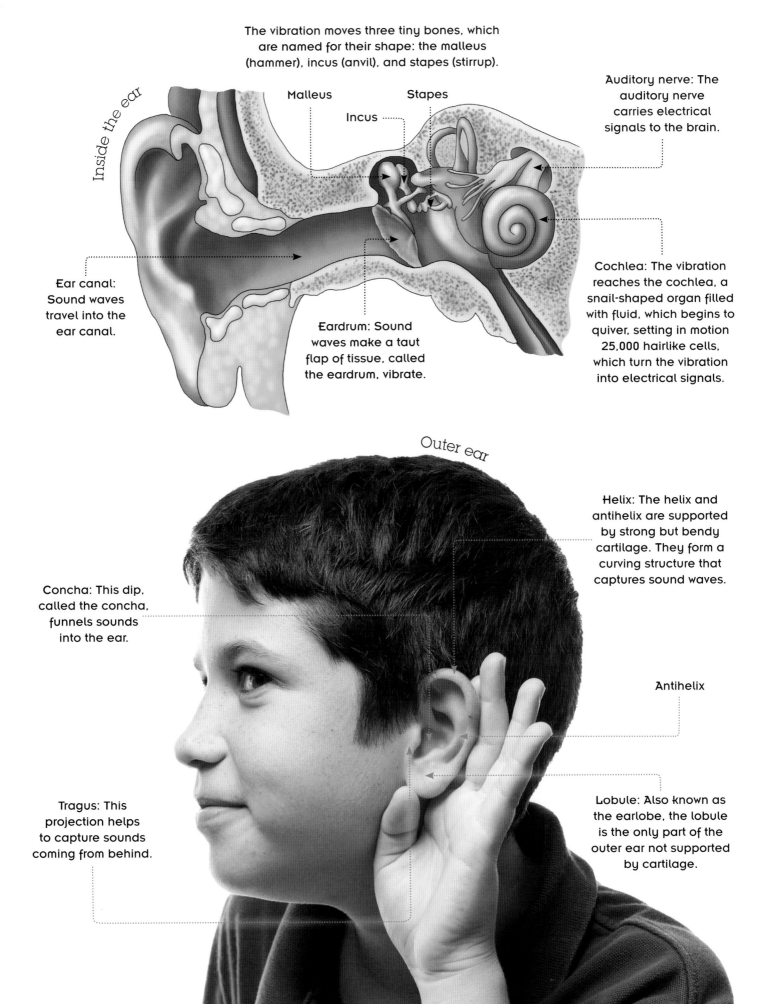

The vibration moves three tiny bones, which are named for their shape: the malleus (hammer), incus (anvil), and stapes (stirrup).

Inside the ear

Malleus

Incus

Stapes

Auditory nerve: The auditory nerve carries electrical signals to the brain.

Ear canal: Sound waves travel into the ear canal.

Eardrum: Sound waves make a taut flap of tissue, called the eardrum, vibrate.

Cochlea: The vibration reaches the cochlea, a snail-shaped organ filled with fluid, which begins to quiver, setting in motion 25,000 hairlike cells, which turn the vibration into electrical signals.

Outer ear

Helix: The helix and antihelix are supported by strong but bendy cartilage. They form a curving structure that captures sound waves.

Concha: This dip, called the concha, funnels sounds into the ear.

Antihelix

Tragus: This projection helps to capture sounds coming from behind.

Lobule: Also known as the earlobe, the lobule is the only part of the outer ear not supported by cartilage.

BALANCE

Your sense of balance stops you from falling over when you are standing or moving. To keep you balanced, your brain processes signals from the inner ear, from the eyes, and from the muscles and joints (see page 110).

The region of the ear that helps with balance is called the vestibular system. This has two key parts: the semicircular canals and the otolith organs. The semicircular canals detect turning movements. The otolith organs detect tilt of the head and acceleration, or speeding up. Signals from these organs are sent both to the brain's cerebellum (which smooths movement) and the cerebrum (which commands movement). The brain interprets these signals and sends commands to adjust the body's movement and posture to maintain balance. The brain also adjusts your eye movements, so that your eyes move in the opposite direction to head movement, keeping your vision steady and unblurred.

Inside an otolith organ

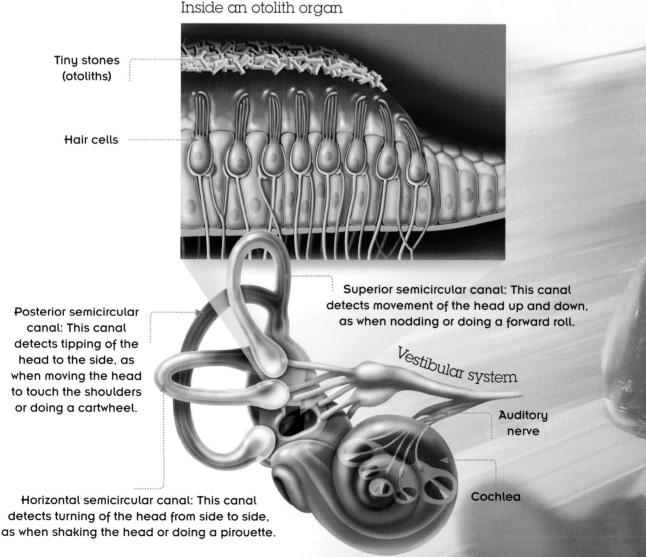

Tiny stones (otoliths)

Hair cells

Superior semicircular canal: This canal detects movement of the head up and down, as when nodding or doing a forward roll.

Posterior semicircular canal: This canal detects tipping of the head to the side, as when moving the head to touch the shoulders or doing a cartwheel.

Vestibular system

Auditory nerve

Cochlea

Horizontal semicircular canal: This canal detects turning of the head from side to side, as when shaking the head or doing a pirouette.

There are three semicircular canals, facing in three different directions, so the vestibular system can detect turning movement in three dimensions. The canals are filled with fluid. When you move, the fluid moves hairlike cells, which translate the movement into electrical signals that are sent to the brain.

Each of the otolith organs has a sheet of tissue which contains tiny, hard crystals of calcium carbonate, named "otoliths." (Otolith means "ear stone.") The sheet of tissue is supported on hair cells. As you tilt or speed up, the stones put pressure on the hair cells, making them bend. This bending is translated into electrical signals. As you descend in an elevator, it is your otoliths that give you the sense you are moving.

When you spin, the fluid in the semicircular canals sloshes around, telling your brain about your rotation. When you stop spinning, the fluid continues sloshing for a few seconds, telling your brain you are moving when you are not. This creates a feeling of dizziness.

Touch receptors in the skin send signals about the pressure, texture, and temperature of the dog. The brain not only understands the dog's shape, furriness, and warmth but generates happy feelings in response to the gentle touch.

TOUCH

Your sense of touch makes use of receptors in your skin, which collect information not just about touch but about pain and temperature, too. Touch is not just important for understanding the world: Kindly touch also comforts us.

A group of receptors that are called mechanoreceptors respond to different types of touch. The most sensitive are Merkel's disks and Meissner's corpuscles, in the top layers of skin. They are found in large numbers on the palms, fingertips, soles of the feet, lips, tongue, and face, making these body parts very sensitive. Merkel's disks are good at sensing continuous pressure and coarse textures. Meissner's corpuscles are good at sensing vibration and fine textures. Deeper in the skin and along joints and muscles are Ruffini's corpuscles and Pacinian corpuscles. They sense deep vibrations and the stretching of skin, which is helpful during activities such as catching a ball.

Receptors that are called thermoreceptors respond to temperature. Both hot and cold receptors are found in the skin all over the body but are in highest numbers on the face and ears, which is why these areas feel cold most quickly. Cold receptors stop sending signals when skin temperature drops below 5 °C (41 °F), giving a feeling of numbness.

You have over 3 million pain receptors, in your skin, muscles, bones, blood vessels, and organs. Pain receptors in the skin create a sharp pain in response to cuts, scrapes, and burns, making you move away from the source of pain immediately. Pain receptors can also create a dull ache to remind you of a bruise or sprain so you rest the damaged area until it heals.

There are four main kinds of mechanoreceptors in the skin.

Meissner's corpuscle

Pacinian corpuscle

Ruffini's corpuscle

Merkel's disks

Meissner's corpuscle

Average size: 0.0085 cm (0.003 in) long

Main functions: Detecting light touch, fine texture, and gentle vibrations

Body system: Nervous

Medical breakthrough: Meissner's corpuscles are the mechanoreceptors that enable people with visual impairments to read Braille using their fingertips. This system of writing was invented by Frenchman Louis Braille in 1824.

Braille uses patterns of tiny bumps to represent letters, numbers, and punctuation.

VOICE BOX

Like all sounds, your voice—whether speaking, shouting, or singing—is made by vibrations (see page 116). You speak by breathing air through the cords of your voice box, also known as the larynx, making them vibrate.

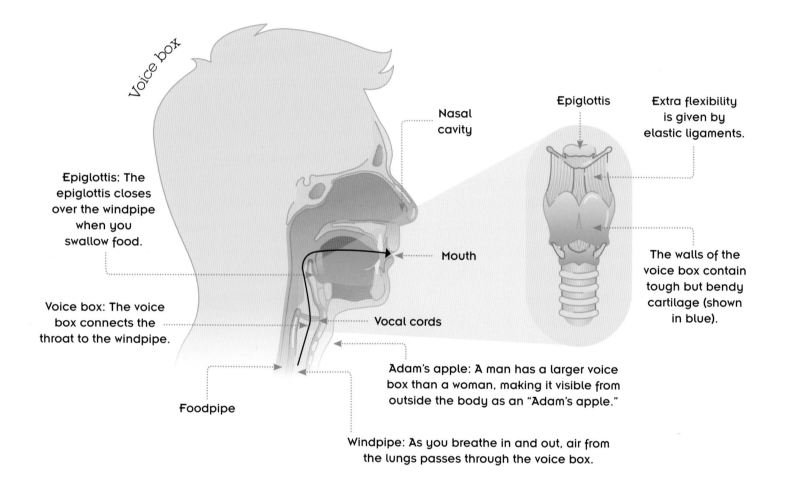

Voice box

Epiglottis: The epiglottis closes over the windpipe when you swallow food.

Voice box: The voice box connects the throat to the windpipe.

Foodpipe

Nasal cavity

Mouth

Vocal cords

Epiglottis

Extra flexibility is given by elastic ligaments.

The walls of the voice box contain tough but bendy cartilage (shown in blue).

Adam's apple: A man has a larger voice box than a woman, making it visible from outside the body as an "Adam's apple."

Windpipe: As you breathe in and out, air from the lungs passes through the voice box.

Voice box

Average size: 4.5 cm (1.8 in) long

Main functions: Enabling speech, letting air pass to and from the windpipe when breathing, and preventing food from entering the windpipe

Body system: Respiratory

Medical breakthrough: Very rarely, someone has their voice box removed because of injury or disease. In 1998, the first larynx transplant was performed successfully.

An electrolarynx is a handheld machine that creates sound by vibrating, enabling someone without a voice box to speak by moving their lips and tongue.

Vocal cords

Vocal cords

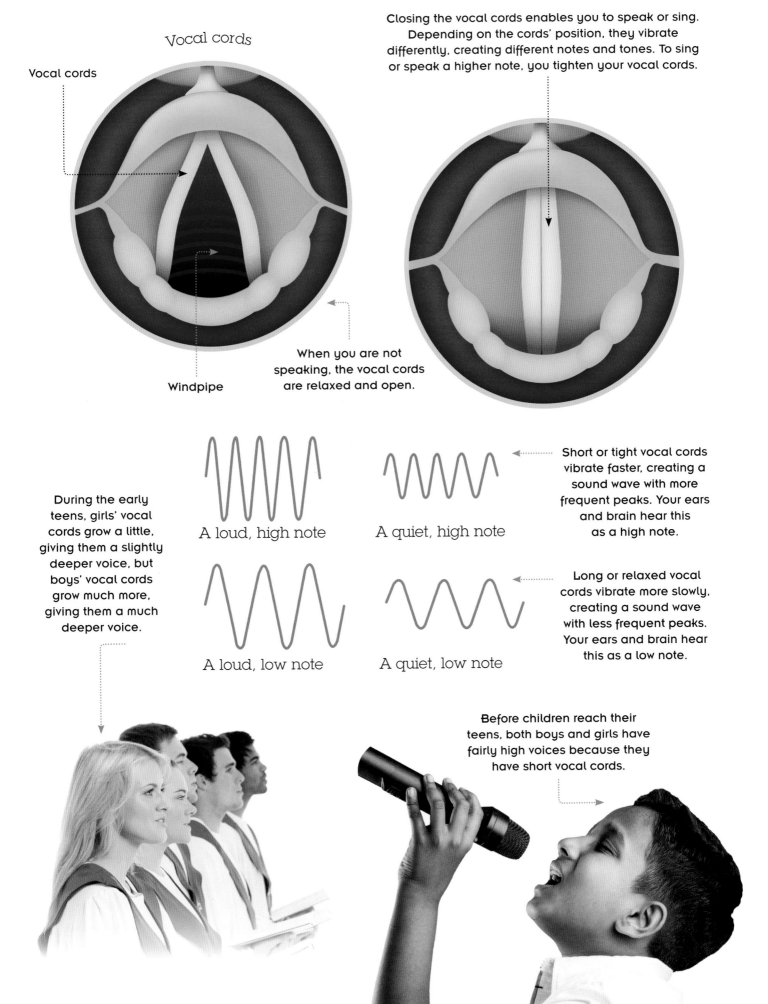

Windpipe

When you are not speaking, the vocal cords are relaxed and open.

Closing the vocal cords enables you to speak or sing. Depending on the cords' position, they vibrate differently, creating different notes and tones. To sing or speak a higher note, you tighten your vocal cords.

A loud, high note

A quiet, high note

A loud, low note

A quiet, low note

Short or tight vocal cords vibrate faster, creating a sound wave with more frequent peaks. Your ears and brain hear this as a high note.

Long or relaxed vocal cords vibrate more slowly, creating a sound wave with less frequent peaks. Your ears and brain hear this as a low note.

During the early teens, girls' vocal cords grow a little, giving them a slightly deeper voice, but boys' vocal cords grow much more, giving them a much deeper voice.

Before children reach their teens, both boys and girls have fairly high voices because they have short vocal cords.

LANGUAGE

Language is the way we share information, ideas, and feelings. Most people learn to speak and understand a spoken language. We also communicate with others using body language, which includes posture, facial expression, and touch. People who are deaf can also communicate using sign languages, which use movements rather than sounds.

There are around 6,000 spoken languages. The majority of people learn their first language from their family or community. Learning a spoken language involves several different areas of the brain, which together co-ordinate breathing, movements of the mouth and vocal cords, memory of words and grammar, and the ability to link a word with the thing it describes (see page 92). Spoken languages use sounds, called phonemes, to form words. Phonemes are made using the breath and voice box, as well as movements of the tongue and lips. The language with the most phonemes is Ta'a, spoken in parts of Botswana and Namibia. Its 161 phonemes include clicking sounds, made by the tongue against the roof of the mouth. English has around 44 phonemes.

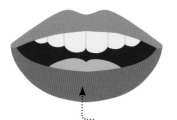

The sound for "e" is made with the mouth open and the tongue behind the bottom teeth.

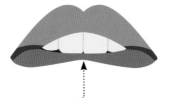

An "f" sound is made with the top teeth touching the bottom lip.

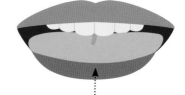

To make a "th" sound, place the tip of the tongue between the teeth and blow air through.

Sign languages are used by people who are deaf or hearing impaired, people who have difficulties with spoken language, and their families and friends. There are around 150 sign languages, with each country usually having its own language. Sign languages use movements of the hands and arms to express numbers, letters, words, and groups of words. Movements of the body and facial expressions are added as grammar or to express emotion or emphasis.

This posture suggests the person is feeling self-confident.

Sometimes we use body language deliberately, when we choose to nod, smile, give a thumbs-up, or pat a shoulder. While most of these movements have the same meaning all over the world, some have different meanings in different cultures. For example, shaking the head from side to side signals disagreement in most countries, but in Bulgaria it means agreement. Much of our body language is unconscious: We communicate our feelings without knowing we are doing so. If we feel sad, we often hunch our shoulders and lower our head. If we are interested, we may tip our head to one side.

Folded arms can suggest disagreement, anger, or boredom.

This gesture suggests the person is thinking about an issue they feel negative or worried about.

Around the world, more than 70 million people use sign languages to communicate with family, friends, classmates, and workmates.

GLOSSARY

ABDOMEN The part of the body below the chest and above the hips.

ABSORB To soak up.

ANATOMY The study of the body and its parts.

ANTIGEN A substance, such as a bacterium, that makes the immune system respond.

ARTERY A tube through which blood travels from the heart to the rest of the body.

ATOM The smallest particle of any material that can exist.

BACTERIUM A tiny, simple living thing that can sometimes cause disease.

BLOOD VESSEL A tube that carries blood around the body.

BRAINSTEM The part of the brain at its base, which controls vital body functions.

CANCER A disease in which abnormal ("not normal") cells divide uncontrollably.

CAPILLARY A tiny blood vessel.

CARBON DIOXIDE A gas that is made by cells as a waste product.

CARDIOVASCULAR SYSTEM The organ system that carries blood around the body.

CARTILAGE A firm but bendy tissue.

CELL The smallest living, working part of the body, which forms all tissues and organs.

CEREBELLUM The part of the brain at the back of the skull, which co-ordinates movement.

CEREBRUM The largest part of the brain, which is responsible for thinking and for processing information from the senses.

CHROMOSOME A long, coiled molecule of deoxyribonucleic acid (DNA).

COLLAGEN A strong material found in bones and skin.

CONNECTIVE TISSUE A tissue that links, supports, or separates other tissues or organs.

CONSCIOUSNESS Being aware of and able to respond to our surroundings.

DEOXYRIBONUCLEIC ACID (DNA) A molecule found in cells, which carries instructions for the growth, function, and reproduction of the body.

DIGESTIVE SYSTEM The organ system that breaks down food so it can be used by the body.

DUCT A tube that carries materials the body has made.

ELECTRON MICROSCOPE A machine that uses a beam of particles to make an enlarged image of a tiny object.

ENDOCRINE SYSTEM The organ system that makes and releases hormones, which are chemicals that act as messengers in the body.

ENZYME A substance that brings about change, such as breaking up food into simpler materials.

FUNGUS A simple living thing that feeds on decaying material or on other living things.

GENE A section of deoxyribonucleic acid (DNA) that contains a particular instruction.

GLAND An organ that makes substances, such as sweat or tears.

GLUCOSE A sugar that the body makes from food and is used by cells as energy.

HEMISPHERE One of the two halves (either left or right) of the brain's cerebrum.

NUCLEUS A structure found inside cells which contains deoxyribonucleic acid (DNA).

NEUROTRANSMITTER A chemical made by neurons that enables them to pass on a signal to other neurons or structures.

NEUROSCIENTIST A scientist who studies the brain and nerves.

NEURON A cell found in the brain and nerves that can communicate with other cells.

NERVOUS SYSTEM The organ system that controls everything the body does. Its key organ is the brain.

NERVE A bundle of neurons that carry messages in the form of electrical signals from the brain to the body and from the body to the brain.

MUSCLE A band or bundle of tissue that can contract (shorten) to produce movement.

MOLECULE A group of atoms that are bonded together.

MINERAL A material needed by the body to grow and be well.

MICROORGANISM A living thing too tiny to be seen without a microscope.

KERATINOCYTE A cell that makes the strong material keratin, found in skin, hair, and nails.

IMMUNITY The ability to resist an infection because the immune system already knows how to defend the body against the invader.

IMMUNE SYSTEM The organ system that defends the body against infection.

HYPOTHALAMUS A part of the brain that has a role in releasing hormones and regulating body temperature.

VIRUS A living thing that can reproduce only inside another living thing and can cause disease.

VEIN A tube through which blood travels from the body to the heart.

VALVE A structure that can close a tube or hole so that liquid can flow in only one direction.

TRANSPLANT The process of putting a new organ or tissue into a person's body.

TRANSFUSION The process of putting new blood into a person's body.

TISSUE A group of similar cells that work together.

RESPIRATORY SYSTEM The organ system that takes in oxygen and expels carbon dioxide.

RECEPTOR A cell that responds to heat, light, or other changes.

PROTEIN A type of molecule that carries out roles in the body from transport to messaging.

POSTURE The position in which someone holds their body.

PIGMENT A colored material.

PARASITE A living thing that lives on or inside another living thing.

OXYGEN A gas that is needed by cells to make energy.

ORGAN SYSTEM A group of organs that work together to carry out particular jobs.

ORGAN A part of the body, made of tissues, that carries out a particular job or jobs.

NUTRIENT A material needed by the body for life and growth.

INDEX